S0-ABT-471

THE

SUPERINTENDENT

PLANS HIS WORK

By Idris W. Jones

VALLEY FORGE

JUDSON PRESS®

© THE JUDSON PRESS 1956

All rights in this book are reserved. No part of the text may be reproduced in any manner without permission in writing from the publisher, except in the case of brief quotations included in a review of the book in a magazine or newspaper.

Except where indicated otherwise, the Bible quotations in this volume are in accordance with the Revised Standard Version of the Bible, copyright 1946 and 1952, by the Division of Christian Education of the National Council of the Churches of Christ in the United States of America, and are used by permission.

ISBN 0-8170-0172-7

LIBRARY OF CONGRESS CATALOG CARD NO. 56-13457

Fourteenth Printing, 1981

JUDSON PRESS

VALLEY FORGE, PA.

The name JUDSON PRESS is registered as a trademark in the U.S. Patent Office. Printed in the U.S.A. ⊕

CONTENTS

1

OBJECTIVE OF CHRISTIAN EDUCATION

The objective of the church's educational ministry is that all persons be aware of God through his self disclosure,

especially his redeeming love as revealed in Jesus Christ;

and, enabled by the Holy Spirit, respond in faith and love,

that as new persons in Christ they may know who they are and what their human situation means; grow as sons of God, rooted in the Christian community; live in obedience to the will of God in every relationship; fulfill their common vocation in the world; and abide in the Christian hope.

Chapter 1

THE GENERAL SUPERINTENDENT
VIEWS HIS WORK

EVERY CHURCH *wants* a good Sunday church school. What is more, every church, no matter how large or how small, can *have* a good Sunday church school. But if it is to have such a school, it must put forth the effort that is required.

Many factors enter into the building of a good Sunday church school, but the key factor is the superintendent. The church, or its board of Christian education, may plan a splendid program to be achieved through its Sunday church school; it may analyze the opportunities for enlisting, training, and equipping teachers; and it may face questions as to curriculum, grading, time schedules, and space allotment. But it still will need a good executive to unify its policies, to see that they are carried out, and to evaluate their effectiveness. The superintendent is that executive, and he will at all times work in close co-operation with the board and the other persons associated with him. The general superintendent is usually elected by the church. Whether the school is large or small, he has executive responsibilities in connection with pupils, teachers, curriculum, space, equipment, and executive staff. These create both his problems and his opportunities.

In most churches the Sunday church school is the principal phase of the Christian education program. In some churches it is the only organized program of Christian education. The leadership of such an organization, therefore, carries a most strategic responsibility.

The superintendent is a key person not only because he carries an important administrative load, but also because he influences the spiritual growth of many persons. His life, his character, and his personal relationships with his officers and teachers have a direct bearing upon their development and morale. His influence upon the pupils comes through a dual channel: directly, through his personal relationships with them; indirectly, through his influence upon their teachers. Thus, the superintendent is a key person both as an executive and as a spiritual leader. The person chosen by the church for this work receives the church's stamp of confidence as an administrator and as an example of the kind of Christian life in which it believes.

The superintendency demands certain other qualifications. Inasmuch as most of them grow out of the nature of the work the superintendent is called upon to perform, let us examine first his task. In a sense, the work is not set before him; it rather moves before him like a constantly changing stream. He usually is summoned to plunge in where the problems are thickest. He will soon discover the problems for himself, if he has not already been briefed concerning them by the pastor, director of Christian education, board of Christian education, or other informed persons. Although conditions will vary from school to school, the superintendent will find that most of his work falls within a framework of duties common to all superintendents.

There are many superintendents who have caught the thrilling vision of their opportunity, who have grasped its elements, and have learned the dual art of "doing first things first" and "assigning responsibility."

THE SUPERINTENDENT'S WORK

The superintendent will note that involved in the nature of his work are six major elements. These are pupils, teachers, curriculum, equipment and space, administrative relationships, and the school's relationships with the church, parents, and community. Whether a school has twenty-five members

```
┌─────────────────────────────────────────────┐
│                                               │
│        THE SUPERINTENDENT'S WORK              │
│                                               │
│                  involves                     │
│                                               │
│                  PUPILS                       │
│                 TEACHERS                      │
│                CURRICULUM                     │
│            EQUIPMENT AND SPACE                │
│        ADMINISTRATIVE RELATIONSHIPS           │
│          THE SCHOOL'S RELATIONSHIPS           │
│                                               │
│                                               │
└─────────────────────────────────────────────┘
```

or two thousand members, these six elements are always present. They call for separate consideration.

1. *Pupils:* The Sunday church school exists for the winning of pupils to Christ and for their training as Christians. Without pupils, no school has any reason for being. Pupils, therefore, are the superintendent's first concern.

In working with pupils, the superintendent is confronted with these questions:

a. How can we find and enlist new pupils?

b. How can we welcome these new members so that they will want to continue coming?

c. How should our pupils be graded?

d. How can we increase regularity of attendance on the part of those who are members?

e. How can we win pupils to an acceptance of Jesus Christ as Lord and Savior?

f. How can we develop churchmanship in the pupils?

g. How can we evaluate the influence of the school upon the pupils?

2. *Teachers:* If a school cannot exist without pupils to be taught, pupils cannot be taught without teachers to instruct them and guide them in their spiritual growth. The securing of teachers, therefore, will always be one of the superintendent's major concerns. Even if his school is fully staffed for the present, he needs to be concerned with the training of available personnel for the future. The superintendent will work with the board of Christian education in the enlistment and development of workers.

The teaching staff, as a factor in the superintendent's work, presents these questions:

a. How many teachers do we need and for what age groups do we need them?
b. Where can we find such present or potential teachers?
c. How can we enlist these persons as teachers?
d. How can we help them to enjoy their work and to grow in effectiveness as teachers?

3. *Curriculum:* The teaching tripod rests on three legs: the pupil, the teacher, and that which is taught—the curriculum. Between what the teacher is consciously attempting to teach and what the pupil actually learns there may be a great chasm. This chasm can be bridged in two ways: through the improved effectiveness of the teacher as a Christian leader, and through the provision of better curriculum materials.

The following questions have to do with the curriculum. The superintendent will find it helpful to discuss them with the teachers, the department superintendents, and the board of Christian education.

a. What are our Christian education goals and objectives, and what do we want to have happen in the lives of our pupils?
b. What curriculum materials can best help us to achieve these Christian education goals?

c. Is our Sunday church school curriculum integrated, or at least correlated, with the other Christian experiences of the pupils?

d. What place does the curriculum give to decision and growth in the Christian life?

e. How effectively is the Bible study, worship, fellowship, and service related to the curriculum objectives?

f. Does the total curriculum include such varied experiences as will provide for growth from department to department, avoid duplication, and prevent the omission of important emphases in the program?

4. *Equipment and Space:* Although the pupil, teacher, and curriculum are the basic elements in the teaching-learning experience, the superintendent will soon discover that other factors become important as the number of teaching-learning groups increases. When one or more new classes are created, the finding of adequate space and equipment may become a major administrative concern. In many churches the board of Christian education is rightly responsible for the allocation of space and the providing of needed equipment. But even where this is the case, the superintendent, as the school executive and an ex-officio member of the board, will be greatly concerned in all decisions relating to space and equipment. These, then, are the questions which the superintendent needs to ask:

a. What is the best use of the existing space and equipment for effective teaching, particularly as that use affects the grading of pupils and the teaching opportunity?

b. What are the points of greatest need in equipment and space?

c. What practical solutions for these needs can the superintendent seek to achieve? What is needed first and how can it be procured?

d. What procedure should he use to see that the school's rooms and equipment are always kept clean and in order?

5. *The Superintendent's Administrative Relationships:* In a small Sunday church school the superintendent's administrative relationships are relatively simple; in a larger school

they are highly complex; in both situations they are exceedingly important. Concerning these administrative relationships the superintendent will find it helpful to ask the following questions:

a. What persons are involved in making decisions affecting our Sunday church school?

b. What is my relationship as superintendent to each of these persons or groups?

c. What is the best distribution of administrative responsibility for our school? What officers do we need?

d. How frequently and on what matters should I, as superintendent, confer with the pastor, the director of Christian education (where one is employed), the board of Christian education, and the teachers and officers of the school?

e. In what way can I best guide the planning of an effective program for our school and help in the assignment of responsibilities?

f. How can I best guide our teachers and officers in setting and achieving annual goals or objectives?

g. How can the program and the classes within the school best be integrated as to time schedules, space, and equipment?

h. How can the program of the Sunday church school best be integrated with the program of the total church and the related activities outside the church?

i. How can I keep a constant check on the program and work of the school in the light of its avowed objectives?

j. What is the nature and frequency of my report as superintendent to the church or to its board of Christian education?

k. On what occasions in church and community am I as superintendent expected to represent the school officially?

l. On what occasions do I act as the presiding officer? How can I become more effective in this responsibility?

6. *The Relationship of the Sunday Church School to the Church, the Parents, and the Community:* The church is constantly teaching through its many activities, even in those cases where it consciously considers its Sunday church school as its only organized educational program. The school actually

is but one part of that wider religious training and experience which the church provides. As the school functions, its members and leaders discover that the total church, the parents of the children and young people, and the community at large—all have an influence on the school, its personnel, and its program.

The superintendent, therefore, can strengthen his school by finding constructive answers to these questions:

a. How can the church as a whole be brought to recognize the value of the Sunday church school and the importance of its teaching program?

b. How can the work and the needs of the school be kept constantly before the church?

c. In what ways do the parents and the school co-operate in the Christian teaching program of the church?

d. What opportunities do the school and its staff have for co-operating with those from other Sunday church schools in training, service, and fellowship?

e. How can the resources of the community be used to advantage in the Sunday church school?

THE SUPERINTENDENT'S LEADERSHIP

As the administrator of the Sunday church school, the superintendent will find himself cast in several roles. By temperament and training he may feel himself better suited for some of these roles than for others. Nevertheless, all of them contribute to his effectiveness. Even in those cases where he may be able to delegate some of these duties to others, an elementary understanding of them will be useful to him. Here we are thinking of the superintendent as a volunteer worker who dedicates his time and ability to the educational work of the church for a period of time—even as many of his fellow workers are serving the church as teachers, department superintendents, youth leaders, deacons, or trustees.

1. *A Spiritual Leader:* When a person is chosen as the superintendent of the Sunday church school, he is by virtue of that choice recognized as a spiritual leader. He may be modest and genuinely humble in spirit, but he becomes, none the less, a spiritual leader. His teachers and officers and pupils will expect him to maintain the spiritual morale of the school by his personal example and by the manner in which he leads.

The superintendent of a large Sunday church school expressed it thus to the writer: "A superintendent, it seems to me, must first of all consecrate himself to the responsi-

---

THE SUPERINTENDENT

is

A SPIRITUAL LEADER

AN EDUCATOR

AN EXECUTIVE

AN ORGANIZER

A LEADER OF WORSHIP

A PERSONAL COUNSELOR

A SYMBOL

---

bility which he has agreed to accept. He must be willing to assume every task, every demand, in connection with his position. He must approach his job with the idea in mind that to further the Christian faith through the position of perintendent is a privilege—not merely a duty. He must spect the high calling of his position and devote his nergies and talents to doing the very best he knows how. econd-best will result in a mediocre school. This, then, eans that a superintendent must first look to himself to e if his motives, his sincerity, his willingness to conserate himself are really genuine and in line with Christian rinciples."

2. *An Educator:* The superintendent is not only a spiritual ader but also an educator. As the superintendent of an ducational organization of the church, he will do well to arn all that he can about the educational process. What good teaching? What is poor teaching? What makes the ifference? What is more important than price in the choice f curriculum materials?

As the superintendent confers with his teachers, he will nd that the more he knows about teaching and its principles, the better he will be able to help them and thus rengthen the morale of his school. Furthermore, an acuaintance with the principles of good teaching will prove elpful to him in many other ways. Some who are called pon to be superintendents do not have the opportunity to ke extensive training as educators. Nevertheless, there are any things they can do to improve their leadership.

Frequently the superintendent will know persons in his hurch or community who have done outstanding work in aching children, youth, or adults. Usually they will be ady to help not only in training teachers, but also in sharng educational insights that will assist the superintendent.

The superintendent can get help from such a book as *each Me to Teach,* by Dorothy B. Swain.[1] This book reflects he objective of the church's educational ministry as develped by many denominations through the Cooperative Curiculum Project. Help also may be found in the departmental
Published by Judson Press, Valley Forge, Pa.

manuals on methods of teaching for nursery, kindergarte, primary, middler, junior, junior high, senior high, olde youth, and adults. Each of these has a bibliography that wi help the ambitious superintendent to grow as an educator.

3. *An Executive:* The superintendent is an executive r sponsible for carrying out the educational policies which a related to the work of the Sunday church school. Part his responsibility is to meet with the board of Christia education, the pastor or church director of Christian educ tion, and the Sunday church school workers for the plannin of policies and program. The co-ordination of time schedul and the best use of available space and equipment are son of his concerns. As a good executive he will plan for ever situation. For example, he will make sure that there a sufficient Bibles, suitable hymnals, and adequate curriculu materials. He will see to it that his teachers and worke know from whom they can secure other supplies, such paper, crayons, and pencils.

As a good executive he will not only plan his own wor but also help his teachers to see the importance of adequa planning for each session of the school. Through his e ample, as well as through his suggestions, he will lead h teachers to discover the thrill of better teaching achieve through proper planning.

4. *An Organizer:* The superintendent is not only an exec tive fulfilling his responsibilities within an organization framework already established, but also he often is a organizer confronted with new responsibilities.

For example, a rural Sunday church school of approx mately fifty members, in one of the midwestern states, ha gone along for years with two children's classes, a yout class, and an adult class. In the 1940's, a nearby city bega to grow! it stretched out until by the end of the decade th church was no longer rural but suburban. For some of th members this was a difficult adjustment. Fortunately, hov

14

ver, both the pastor and the superintendent were men of ision. Instead of permitting the school to grow in hit-or-iiss fashion, adding a class whenever the current pressure illed for it, they reorganized the school on a graded basis iat would allow for all foreseeable expansion. This grow-ig church now has a board of Christian education in charge f all its educational activities, and the church itself is work-ig to find additional space for its increased membership.

Few superintendents will run into such a major organi-itional change; but for those who do, the staff members f the national and area Christian education offices stand ady to help.

The superintendent's work as an organizer will often have do with the inauguration of some new program or the rganization of some new group within the existing Sunday urch school. To launch the new program or group success-lly, the superintendent will find it helpful to keep several rinciples in mind:

a. The greatest possible number of the persons affected, directly indirectly, should be shown the need for the new venture.

b. The greatest possible number of those essential to the success the venture should be given the chance to share in determining nature and process of realization.

c. A well-planned time schedule should be prepared for the hievement of the new program or group.

d. Responsibility for specific tasks contributing to the success of e new venture should be assigned to and accepted by the appro-iate persons or groups.

e. The new venture should be launched enthusiastically. The ason for it, the results to be achieved through it, and the need for support should be thoroughly publicized.

5. *A Leader of Worship:* A unified Sunday program of orship and study deserves consideration by our Sunday urch schools. The increase in teaching time and the elimi-tion of duplication are only two of its many values. For

churches with a unified program of worship and study, th
church service of worship becomes the worship assembl
of the school as well. Any additional worship experienc
within the school's time is usually in the children's or yout
division on a graded basis.

In some Sunday church schools the superintendent i
directly responsible for the leadership of worship; in othe
schools he may counsel other persons in the leadership c
worship. Although he will depend greatly on the pastor c
church director of Christian education for help in this field
he can become a more competent leader through learnin
and using the basic principles of public and graded worship
One of the sections of the school library should be made u
of worship resource materials.

6. *A Personal Counselor:* Any person in an administra
tive position soon becomes aware that the personal prob
lems of those working under his leadership affect thei
competence within his organization. This is as true of Sun
day church school workers as of others. Many of these prob
lems the superintendent will want to refer to the pastor c
some other competent person. In all cases, however, th
superintendent will be a better leader if his workers fee
they can discuss with him their personal problems as the
affect their church school work. If they realize that the
disclosures will be treated confidentially and with good jud
ment, he will find a growing rapport with his workers.

The superintendent should by no means seek to serve a
a professional counselor, but a willingness to listen, a stri
keeping of confidences, and a genuine Christian concern fc
the discovery of avenues of helpfulness, will strengthen hi
in the leadership of his staff.

7. *A Symbol:* As the leader of the Sunday church schoo
the superintendent is in many ways a symbol—a symbol c
the school. Within the church fellowship as well as in th
community and elsewhere he represents the school. Withi

the school itself he is a symbol to both pupils and teachers. If it is a strong school, he is a symbol of its strength and achievements; if it is a weak and ineffective school, he is a symbol of that weakness. As the minister is for many the representative of the church which he serves, so the superintendent is identified with the nature and quality of the school which he leads.

THE SUPERINTENDENT'S GROWTH

As the superintendent looks at his task and considers the nature of the leadership he is called upon to give, he may well be thankful that he does not face his task in his own strength only. For support he can call on his pastor, the church as a whole, and his fellow workers within the Sunday church school. Supremely, however, he will be aware that he is one who is working together with God in the achievement of Christian education objectives within the lives of the members of his school. If there are times when he doubts his ability to carry out some of his responsibilities, he can read with renewing confidence the comment of Paul to the Corinthian church: "We have this treasure in earthen vessels, to show that the transcendent power belongs to God and not to us" (2 Cor. 4:7).

No truly competent superintendent will ever feel that he is completely adequate for all the phases of his work. Therefore, he will seek constantly to grow both in his understanding of his work and in his ability to do it. Some ways through which this growth can be aided are:

1. *Study of Christian Education Magazines and Books:* Magazines published by his own denomination offer a rich source of help. Some of the articles concern small schools, some concern large schools, but all of them are of value regardless of the size of the school. Some of these articles the superintendent will refer to other workers within

17

the school. He will do well, however, to be conversant with their contents.

A constant stream of excellent books on Christian education comes from the presses these days. They differ in quality, of course, and the superintendent will have to decide which he will read. The personal recommendation of someone in whom he has confidence, a careful analysis of the descriptive material advertising the new books, or the recognition of a personal need may lead to his choice of specific books. By studying even one carefully chosen book each quarter (four books a year) the superintendent will grow measurably in his understanding of his task and of the ways by which he can perform it.

2. *Attendance at Training Schools and Conferences:* Although individual churches do not find it feasible to organize a study course for general superintendents, an increasing number of communities are doing so. Such a class may be organized on a community-wide, state-wide, or even national basis. Area or national conferences for superintendents are usually scheduled by the denominations. Some denominations provide training by correspondence. Conferences with other superintendents, whether informal or as a part of a training school, can bring inspiration as well as information. The effective superintendent will participate in as many such conferences as his opportunity and time will permit.

3. *Knowledge of the Curriculum Materials and the Teaching Procedures of His Workers:* The superintendent grows not only as he increases his fund of information, but also as he has occasion to test the workability of his knowledge in connection with the opportunities and problems of his school. As he and his workers make use of their materials or seek together the answers to the problems of their school, the superintendent will grow in leadership stature. He will discover that the authority of helpful guidance is much stronger and more enduring than the authority of position—

especially in a volunteer organization such as the Sunday church school.

4. *Spiritual Development:* No one stands still spiritually. Any person in a position of spiritual leadership, such as a superintendent, either becomes increasingly conscious of his relationship to God through prayer, work, Bible study, and devotional reading, or he strains with futility to maintain the semblance of it. The superintendent must truly be a Christian before he can become an effective administrator, educator, or leader. His spiritual condition is basic to everything else he is and does. Prayer and Bible study must be an integral part of his daily life because they will strengthen his awareness of the God whom he serves.

As the superintendent grows, he will find an ever greater thrill in his work and an increasing joy in the doing of it. His is truly an important task that requires not only the dedication of all that he has, but also a willingness to become greater than he is.

QUESTIONS AND PROJECTS

1. What are the qualifications of a good superintendent?

2. Recall two or three situations in which you believe you were helpful to workers whom you counseled.

3. What sort of plan do you have for the improvement of your spiritual life?

4. Make a list of what you think are your responsibilities as superintendent of your Sunday church school. Check those which you have been carrying out. Think of ways by which you can include other duties, in order to increase your effectiveness as a superintendent.

5. Note the six "factors" mentioned in this chapter as being involved in the superintendent's work. Select the factor in which you are weakest, or the one which is most needed in your school, and make a study of it.

Chapter 2

THE TEACHING PROGRAM OF THE
SUNDAY CHURCH SCHOOL

EVERY THOUGHTFUL SUPERINTENDENT will look at his school from time to time with a questioning eye. As he sees the adults, the young people, and the children streaming out of their classes at the close of the session, he may feel satisfaction in the fact that they keep coming Sunday after Sunday. But how much have they been benefited? What ought the school to be achieving in their lives?

A GOOD SUNDAY CHURCH SCHOOL PROGRAM

The Sunday church school has as its primary responsibility the teaching ministry of the church. Other phases of the

---

A GOOD PROGRAM

is

INTEGRATED

GRADED

GROWING

STAFFED

PLANNED

---

church life, of course, have a teaching contribution which they will make to the persons engaging in them; and the members of the school will be expected to participate fully in all the worship, witnessing, service, and fellowship opportunities which the church provides. But a sharing in these other experiences will only partly compensate for the school's shortcomings, if it is weak in its teaching program.

1. *An Integrated Program:* A good Sunday church school program will be an integral part of the total educational effort of the church. In most churches it is the major part. In any case, the church school program should be closely related to the total program of the church. Usually this integration is achieved through a board of Christian education. Such a board is elected by the church to develop and supervise its educational program. The church school superintendent is ex-officio a member of this board; and, therefore, he has a part in determining the educational policies of the church, including those which have to do with the Sunday church school.

2. *A Graded Curriculum:* A good Sunday church school will have a well-balanced and varied curriculum, graded for the age-groups to which the school ministers. The school will be wise to make full use of the curriculum resources and materials provided by its denomination. These materials are based on an intelligent and reverent use of the Bible; they develop a clear understanding of Christian principles; they include evangelistic concern and practice; and they seek to keep the pupils informed as to the program and missionary outreach which their church has through its denomination.

3. *A Growing School:* A good Sunday church school will endeavor to increase each year the number of persons enrolled. To say that a school is more interested in quality than in quantity is a poor excuse for not being interested in both. Usually the school that is interested in both quality

and quantity does better work in both than the school that emphasizes one to the exclusion of the other.

The Sunday church school is still by far the most effective evangelistic arm of the church, for approximately 85 per cent of those who are members of the church have come by way of the Sunday church school. It should continue to be so.

4. *A Trained Staff:* A good Sunday church school will train, support, and give due recognition to its teachers and officers. The responsibility they carry for encouraging Christian decisions and for guiding growth in the Christian life is somewhat overwhelming, but the rewards are great. To do his best work each teacher needs (a) a genuine Christian experience and guidance in growth in it; (b) training and experience in understanding pupils; (c) a knowledge of the objectives of Christian education; (d) training and experience in using good teaching methods; (e) a sound knowledge of the curriculum materials and resources related to his teaching responsibility.

5. *Co-operation in Planning:* A good Sunday church school will plan and evaluate its program in the light of the goals and objectives which have been adopted co-operatively by the board of Christian education and the church school workers, under the leadership of the pastor, the director of Christian education, and the general superintendent.

As an example of goals for a Sunday church school, there is given below the Standard of Achievement which was used for many years by one denomination and proved its worth in thousands of churches—small and large, rural and urban. Although no longer an official standard, its values are still evident, and many schools may find worth in adapting it to their own situations. Such a standard is not to be used once and then forgotten, but should be referred to continually as the standard by which the work of the school is to be judged. It embodies the five basic principles set forth at the beginning of this chapter, and it suggests many tests of effectiveness that make these principles practical.

STANDARD OF ACHIEVEMENT

For Sunday Church Schools

I. ATTENDANCE INCREASE

   A. Average attendance increased at least 5 per cent (the percentage changes after the first year)
   B. The use of a definite plan for the enrollment and conservation of members

II. LEADERSHIP TRAINING

   A. A training program in which 25 per cent of the teachers, department superintendents, and general officers earn one or more Leadership Education credits
   B. A minimum of six Workers' Conferences attended by 60 per cent of the teachers and officers

III. CHURCH LOYALTY

   A. An average of at least 60 per cent of those in attendance above the Primary Department participating in the church's program of Sunday morning worship (the percentage changes after the first year)
   B. Giving to local expenses and to the world missions encouraged through the use of an envelope system in all departments above the Nursery, or through a proportionate share of the weekly offering

IV. BIBLE STUDY

A. The Bible used as the basis for study and worship in every department and class

B. The message of the Bible taught through the use of denominationally recommended teaching materials in every department and class

V. WORLD MISSION

A missionary education program including two of the following:

A. Interpretation of three areas of the denominational program in all groups above the Kindergarten

B. A missionary education library with current books in each department above Kindergarten, and a plan in operation for their use

C. Active participation in a graded church school of missions

VI. COMMUNITY WITNESS

A. A definite plan of visitation to enroll the unreached

B. Completion of one or more projects in Christian social relations

VII. DECISIONS FOR CHRIST

A genuine concern to win all persons to Jesus Christ through:

A. Training teachers to guide their pupils toward a decision for Christ as Lord and Savior

B. Special classes in discipleship and church membership

VIII. SPIRITUAL ENRICHMENT

A. A program to encourage personal and family devotional practices
B. A program for the spiritual growth of teachers and officers

IX. CHURCH-HOME CO-OPERATION

Co-operation with the home in the Christian guidance of pupils in two of the following:

A. One or more visits to the home of every pupil
B. The use of curriculum materials for the home
C. Two or more parent-teacher meetings for co-operative planning

X. EFFECTIVE ORGANIZATION

A. The Sunday church school related to the church through a church-elected board of Christian education
B. An approved plan of grouping and grading

XI. SUMMER ACTIVITIES

A program which includes two of the following:

A. Training opportunities for church school workers
B. Church school members encouraged to take advantage of opportunities in church camping
C. Active participation in a vacation church school

XII. BETTER EQUIPMENT

A. Evaluation of rooms and equipment in relation to pupil needs and formulation of plans for improvement
B. Definite evidence of some improvement each year

The board of Christian education, of which the superintendent is ex-officio a member, is responsible for the educational program of the church. Under its leadership and direction the Sunday church school program will be developed. For this purpose the board will enlist the co-operation not only of the superintendent of the Sunday church school, but also of its teachers and officers. At strategic points, such as the interpretation of curriculum, the changing of time schedules, and the discussion of church school goals and objectives, the church membership should be invited to participate. Such a procedure will bring stability as well as strength to the school, because it is done not merely to receive additional ideas and suggestions, but also to enlist broad participation in the building of a good Sunday church school program. Such participation is both an educational experience and a step toward intelligent and enthusiastic support. The judgment and decision of the board of Christian education will determine the extent to which such participation is enlisted. Certainly the staff of the Sunday church school should have a large part in the development of the program.

1. *Objectives:* In building a good Sunday church school program the first question concerns objectives. What are we trying to accomplish through the total educational program of the church? What is the place of the Sunday church school in accomplishing these objectives?

"Denominations, working together through the International Council of Religious Education, long ago agreed on a general statement of the objectives of Christian education. These objectives have helped program planners to develop program guides. They have helped local church workers to recognize the responsibility which they have for the Christian nurture of persons. . . . Objectives . . . for any church should include such essential elements as: belief in

God and relationship to him, acceptance of Jesus Christ, the Bible, the Church, personal Christian living, the person and his role in society, and a Christian philosophy of life."[1]

These general objectives, with the adaptations made necessary by the various age levels, are achieved through the Christian fellowship of the church in worship, study, service, and witness. Some of these objectives are realized through the Sunday worship services of the church, some through the various group meetings held during the week. Others are achieved most effectively through the Sunday church school.

This study of objectives should result in four improvements:

   a. A clarification of the true objectives of the Sunday church school.

   b. A better understanding of the relationship between the Sunday church school and other organized phases of church life.

   c. A delegation of responsibility to the various groups functioning in church life, such as the Youth Fellowship evening groups, men's and women's organizations, and especially, the Sunday church school.

   d. The elimination of irrelevant or harmful customs, and the strengthening of practices which promote the true objectives of the school.

2. *Analysis:* When a thorough study has been made of the objectives of Christian education and of the responsibilities of the Sunday church school in their realization, the next step involves an analysis of the present school activities and program for children, youth, and adults:

   a. What age groups are we serving through our Sunday church school?
   b. How many persons are reached in each age group?
   c. How effective are these age groups (classes or departments)

[1] *Christian Nurture Through the Church,* by Lee J. Gable. Copyright, 1955, by the National Council of the Churches of Christ in the U.S.A. Used by permission.

in achieving the desired goals and objectives of the Sunday church school in the lives of their members?

d. Which activities or program elements should be eliminated? Which should be strengthened? Which should be added?

3. *Specific Goals:* Clear objectives and a thorough analysis of the present program constitute the groundwork for the building of a good program. These matters must be well studied, if that which is built on them is to be a sound program. Next in order comes the planning of the specific steps by which the improved program is to be achieved. Responsibility for each step must be assigned. Although this can be done at any time, an especially good time is the spring or late summer. Out of such a planning session can come long-term objectives, as well as specific goals for the coming year.

In planning specific steps for the immediate present and for the long-term future, answers to the following questions should prove helpful.

PROGRAM BUILDING

calls for

GOALS

SCHEDULE

RESPONSIBILITY

RESOURCES

INFORMED MEMBERSHIP

PERIODIC CHECK-UP

---

a. In the light of our general objectives and of our present program, what are our most urgent needs?

b. What specific goals should grow out of these needs?

c. When should these goals be realized?

d. Who is responsible for the fulfillment of each specific goal?

e. What resources are available?

f. How can we keep our church and community informed as to our objectives and achievements?

By way of answers to these questions, the following comments will be in order. They refer to the questions in turn.

The more urgent needs, on investigation, may be found to relate to the curriculum, the teachers, the training of leaders, the equipment and room arrangement, the outreach to new pupils, or the relationship of the church school to other parts of the church program.

Some of these needs can be met easily and quickly. These should be assigned to the appropriate persons for attention within a specified time. From the remaining suggestions should be chosen those that seem the more urgent.

At this point the group should proceed with wisdom and faith; wisdom in choosing goals possible of achievement; faith in selecting goals that will require dedicated time, ability, and energy to achieve. Furthermore, these goals should be specific. How much of an increase in enrollment, for example, should be sought during the next year and how shall it be obtained? How shall regularity of attendance be promoted? What new classes need to be set up, if the school is to minister to all ages effectively? Does any class need to be shifted to a different room to provide more adequate space for all? What kinds of leadership training should be organized? How many present and prospective teachers should we strive to enlist in these training classes? The answers to these and other questions should be expressed in the goals adopted.

By what date are these goals to be achieved? A four- or five-year program of development, expressed in long-term goals, is a valuable guide for any Sunday church school. Every school, however, will do well to set up some goals on an annual basis. These may be complete in themselves or they may be steps in the achievement of a comprehensive five-year goal.

In this connection the Sunday church school calendar for the year should be examined and its principal dates noted. The schedule for the achievement of these goals will need to be integrated with the continuing calendar of the school. A change of class rooms, for example, might take place in September or October, while a leadership school might be held in October-November or January-February. If a leadership class for training prospective workers is held during the Sunday morning church school session, it should be held during those months when special all-school programs will not interfere with it.

As an annual recognition of the past year's attainments Ross and McRae in *The Superintendent Faces His Task* suggest the use of an annual "Achievement Day." On this occasion the goals of the past year are reviewed and the successes and failures are noted. Such an emphasis serves as a spur to achievement and as a stimulus to morale, provided that the goals are a true challenge and the successes are noteworthy. The June workers' conference or Christian Education Week might serve the purpose of such an "Achievement Day." In any case, the whole church should be informed both as to the goals and as to the results attained.

Assignment of responsibility, of course, is an important step in the fulfillment of any objective. Certain persons by virtue of their committee or staff designations automatically become responsible for certain goals. Even so, the specific

[1] *The Superintendent Faces His Task,* by Charles M. Ross and Glenn McRae. The Bethany Press, Saint Louis.

ssignments should be indicated and their consent secured to ssume these responsibilities as part of their continuing work.

It is equally important to give due recognition to those /ho have carried responsibility to successful completion. To ssign responsibility, to secure consent, to recognize achieve-nent—these are three important steps in stimulating full ersonal effort.

Fortunately, no church has to meet its Christian teaching eeds without help. In addition to those resources which very church has within itself or within its community, de-ominational offices, area or national, frequently can be of ssistance. They not only can give counsel with respect to urriculum materials, but also render many other services /hich the denominations make available. These will be dis-ussed more fully in a later section of this chapter.

It is important that the Sunday church school keep both the hurch and the community informed as to its objectives and chievements. Such publicity makes it easier to enlist addi-ional persons in the program, and it inspires those already haring in it to participate more wholeheartedly.

The best form of publicity, of course, is the contagious nthusiasm of those who feel that they are participating in worthy teaching program. In addition, the goals, achieve-nents, and values of the Sunday church school should be ontinuously brought to the attention of the potential con-tituency. The annual "Achievement Day" provides an excel-ent opportunity to do this, but it should be supplemented hrough more frequent publicity. The weekly or monthly hurch paper, if the church has one, should provide space 1 which the activities and progress of the school may be oted. From time to time, when the occasion merits it, letters hould go out to the constituency informing them concerning ome major event. The co-operation of the pastor should e enlisted in keeping the work of the school before the nembers of the church. Newspapers will print newsworthy

31

items. These will keep the community aware of the value of the church school, and will strengthen the conviction of those sharing in the school that they are part of a significant organization.

It is not wise to wait until near the end of the year to see how well the year's objectives are being achieved. More frequent check-up is advisable. One school, for example, uses part of its workers' conference each month for a brief review of its goals and a noting of results to date. Thus there is presented an opportunity to remedy laxity and to encourage school progress.

TEACHING MATERIALS

As previously stated, the teaching experience in its most elementary form involves three things: pupils, teacher, and that which is taught and learned. The materials, therefore, which the teacher uses as an aid to teaching and those the pupil uses as an aid to learning are of strategic importance. In choosing teaching materials, five criteria of good teaching materials are suggested:

1. *Biblical:* The Bible is basic to our teaching. All teaching materials, therefore, should display a reverent use of the Bible and an intelligent understanding of its message and central worth.

2. *Denominational:* The pupils should be informed as to the distinctive principles for which their denomination stands; they should be aware of the nature and extent of their world-wide mission.

3. *Evangelistic:* A decision for Christ as Lord and Savior, responsible participation in the life of the church, and a full Christian witness in vocational and community life should be the experience of every person enlisted in the school. Such a purpose should motivate the school's teaching program and it should permeate all of the teaching material used in the school.

```
TEACHING MATERIALS

should be

BIBLICAL
DENOMINATIONAL
EVANGELISTIC
MISSIONARY
GRADED
```

4. *Missionary:* A strong missionary program at home and abroad is imperative. Such missionary effort can be maintained and extended only as church members are inspired by a good understanding of the program. Curriculum materials should aid the teacher in developing the missionary consciousness of the pupils.

5. *Graded:* The experience of growth is God-given. Persons are constantly changing in their interests and understanding from babyhood through adulthood. Classes in the Sunday church school should be graded in age as closely as enrollment and teaching space permit.

Three types of teaching materials are provided for the churches; namely, graded, uniform, and elective.

The Graded Series embodies effective methods of teaching which are graduated to the age level, understanding, and experience of the pupil. The needs and interests of the pupil are brought to the Bible in order that the light of the Word of God may shine upon them. The way is opened for personal response through a variety of learning experiences, practical activities, and day-by-day living.

The Uniform Series starts the lesson with a portion of Scripture, which is then applied to life in terms of the needs of varying groups.

Elective Courses are provided for the purpose of exploring a chosen subject or as an occasional change from the Uniform Lessons.

If special questions arise—possibly at the point of grading classes or in helping teachers make the best use of teaching materials—the superintendent can get in touch with the denominational office.

Rooms and Equipment

Curriculum materials are not the only factor that affects the teaching program of the Sunday church school. Children, youth, and adults alike are affected also by the setting in which the teaching takes place. It is important that they be provided with surroundings that are conducive to learning.

One superintendent claims that 80 per cent of our Sunday church schools have to function with insufficient space and equipment. One thing, however, is certain; no matter how inadequate classroom space may be, it can be kept clean, cheerful, and well ventilated. Dirt and disorder make doubly oppressive an already cramped space; whereas a room that is clean, with floors, chairs, and woodwork dusted, and with walls and ceiling cheerful and free from cobwebs, becomes an invitation to better teaching and learning.

Chairs should be sturdy and comfortable. They should be correctly graded as to size for the age group by which they will be used. Adequate lighting and cheerful but restful colors materially affect both teacher and pupils.

Every church, no matter how large or how small, can improve its teaching program by keeping its rooms clean, well lighted, correctly ventilated, and adequately equipped. Pictures, worship centers, Bibles, blackboards, maps, and hymnals should be kept neat and in a place easy of access. Closets and cabinets are better depositories for such equipment than are open, dust-collecting shelves.

The problem of space, of couse, is frequently a serious one. When all available space is in use, the church may consider two possible solutions. It can remodel its building or build additional rooms. Or it can stagger the Sunday church school department sessions and church worship services. The latter solution may take the following pattern: In the first hour, part of the school studies while the other participates in the church worship service; then, in the second period, the groups are reversed. Or some of the classes might meet before the preaching serivce; other classes might meet following the preaching service. In this way each classroom would be used twice. If a church has only one room and must use it for both its worship and its study session, a graded program presents a challenge, but it is not impossible.

The allocation of rooms for use by the Sunday church school is the responsibility of the board of Christian education. In such decisions by the board, the judgment and suggestions of the superintendent will have a large place. It is wise to review annually the use made of the available classrooms, recognizing that changes in the size or needs of classes may make a shift advisable.

Special equipment is being added by many churches because excellent audio-visual teaching materials are now available to strentghen the teaching program of the church. A basic piece of equipment to make the best use of these materials is a tri-purpose projector which accommodates single or double-frame filmstrips or 2″ x 2″ slides. With the increased number of high quality religious films, a motion picture projector becomes a good investment for many churches. Its initial cost, plus the cost of film rentals, may make it seem quite expensive. In such situations, however, a group of churches, through a council of churches or on their own initiative, may desire to purchase such equipment co-operatively.

THE CHURCH LIBRARY

A church library can be a valuable asset to the Sunday church school. It requires an accessible room, adequate shelves for the attractive display of books and magazines, and an enthusiastic librarian who will not only catlogue the books properly but will also promote the use of the library.

The nature of the library will be determined by the use which the church plans to make of it. There are three broad classifications, any one or all of which may be served by the library: books for church school workers; religious books for parents and children to use in the home; books of general interest to the church membership.

Most churches begin with a library for church school workers, or at least include books for such workers. An item in the Christian education budget should make possible a reasonable number of additions to the library each year. Suggestions for such additions may be found in the denomination's catalogue, or by writing to the Christian Education Department of the denomination.

Equally important is the goal of getting workers to use the library. This can be done through recommending specific books to those persons who will find them helpful. Publicizing recent additions to the library with an explanation of the appeal that led to their choice, and calling attention to two or thee relevant books at each workers' conference, are additional ways of stimulating interest in the library. The library can be a valuable means of training teachers. It should not be neglected!

1. Be prepared to make a three-minute talk or write a page on the importance of the teaching of the Bible as a means of spreading the gospel.

2. Obtain and study the objectives and standards which are recommended by your denomination for the church school program.

3. Make a survey of the materials being used in your Sunday church school and list your findings for each department. Evaluate these findings in the light of the criteria set up by the author. Indicate improvements which you would recommend.

4. Evaluate your present equipment, and on the basis of equipment needs make recommendations for purchases.

Chapter 3

ORGANIZING AND ADMINISTERING THE SUNDAY CHURCH SCHOOL

CHRISTIAN TEACHING, in some form or other, has been a function of the Christian church from its inception. The Sunday church school as we know it today, however, is of more recent origin. It has evolved from an eighteenth-century experiment by a devout Christian layman, Robert Raikes, in teaching boys and girls to read and write. These schools, organized first in England, were designed to help the children who worked long hours in factories on every week day; hence, they met on Sunday and for educational materials they used chiefly the Bible.

These Sunday schools later broadened their program to include religious training for youth and adults. They were held in church buildings, and usually drew upon the members of the church for their teachers and officers. They functioned, however, as separate organizations. Each had administrative autonomy and raised its own budget. From time to time the school made a contribution to the church in return for the use of its facilities. As these Sunday schools grew, they provided many lay persons with an opportunity for Christian service and leadership. As a result of the intimate and informal fellowship in study and teaching they provided, they won the devotion of millions.

During the first half of the twentieth century it was perceived that the teaching responsibility of the church and the purpose of the Sunday school were identical, and there has been a significant effort to make the Sunday school an integral part of the church organization and program. This awakened understanding that Christian teaching is the responsibility of the whole church is revealed in the use of such designations as "the school of the church," "the church school," and "the Sunday church school."

The church school, therefore, is the whole church, as a church, communicating the gospel to children, youth, and adults through the teaching process. This is the concern of the whole church, and is to be achieved through all its program. The Sunday church school, the largest organization for Christian education in the church, is an expression of this purpose. Administratively, therefore, the Sunday church school should be accountable to the church, and the church should be responsible for the effective ministry of the Sunday church school. It is understood, of course, that the church should seek to expand its educational program beyond the Sunday church school to include the vacation church school, the week-day church school, the school of missions, and other Christian education activities.

The true strength of the Sunday church school lies in its enlistment of our finest laymen in the teaching program of the church. The contagion of their dedicated lives and devoted spirit gives power to the Christian truth they seek to communicate. The Sunday church school enables them to share their faith. This they do through what they are and through the help which they give to others.

How Should the School Be Organized?

The organization of the Sunday church school involves two phases: its relationship to the church as a whole and its organization within itself.

1. *The Church at Study:* The Sunday church school is the church at study on Sunday morning. It should be administered, therefore, by the church through its board of Christian education. The general superintendent, as the executive charged with the administration of the school, is an ex-officio

member of the board of Christian education. As such, he will share in the making of all board decisions other than the board's annual nomination to the church of the superintendent for the coming year.

The board of Christian education is responsible for the appointment of all Sunday church school officers and teachers serving under the general superintendent.

The board of Christian education is responsible for organizing leadership education opportunities for the church school staff, and it is expected to enlist new personnel for the leadership of the educational program.

The board of Christian education, through its age-group committees (children, youth, and adult), is concerned with discovering new ways of strengthening the church's educational program within these three age divisions.

The board of Christian education will bring other special resources to the Sunday church school through such committees as those for missionary and stewardship education, leadership education, music, drama, worship, recreation, camping, and audio-visual aids.

Because of his executive responsibilities, the superintendent of the school will serve not only as an ex-officio member of the board of Christian education, but also as an ex-officio member of its subcommittees. Inasmuch as the superintendent is concerned with the general excellence of the school, and is probably the person best informed as to its total needs, he should prove a key member in the work of the board as it relates to the Sunday church school.

2. *The School Pattern:* Within the school itself, the pattern of organization depends in part on the type of educational program the church desires, and in part on the number of persons involved. For example, a school with sixty pupils will probably have six classes: one for preschool children (under 6 years); one for primary children (grades 1, 2; ages 6, 7 approximately); one for middlers (grades 3, 4;

ages 8, 9 approximately); one for juniors (grades 5, 6; ages 10, 11 approximately); one for youth (junior high and senior high); and one for adults. Administratively, such a school would call for six teachers, some associate teachers and helpers, a superintendent, an assistant superintendent, a secretary-treasurer, and a pianist.

At the other extreme, there are churches of such size that their schools will have from five to ten young adult classes and an even larger number of adult classes, with corresponding numbers in the children's and youth divisions. Such schools require many teachers and helpers.

Schools are graded according to the number of pupils. Some standards for grading follow:

a. Nursery Department, made up of children who range in age from birth to three years inclusive. The Nursery Department may be divided, if the numbers warrant, into two groups (birth to third birthday, and a separate group for three-year-olds); into three groups (birth to eighteen months, eighteen months to third birthday, and the three-year-olds); or into four groups (birth to twelve months, one-year-olds, two-year-olds, and three-year-olds). If these divisions still leave more than twelve to fifteen children in any one nursery room, the group should be further divided.

b. Kindergarten Department, made up of children four and five years of age. When the number of kindergarten children exceeds twenty or twenty-five, the department should be divided into a four-year-old group and a five-year-old group. If the resulting age groups are still above twenty to twenty-five members, further division is needed.

c. Primary Department. These children are in public school grades 1, 2 (ages 6, 7 approximately). When the number of children in this group exceeds twelve to fifteen, the group should be divided into classes according to public school grade. If this division still leaves classes exceeding twelve in membership, the large classes should be further divided.

d. Middler (or Lower Junior Department), made up of children in public school grades 3, 4 (ages 8, 9 approximately). The suggestions given for the Primary Department as to divisions into classes also apply to Middlers.

e. Junior Department, made up of children in public school grades 5, 6 (ages 10, 11 approximately). The suggestions given for the Primary Department as to division into classes apply also to Juniors.

f. Junior High Department, grades 7, 8, 9 (ages 12, 13, 14 approximately). When the number in this department exceeds fifteen to twenty, it should be divided for classroom work. A class of five or more Junior High youths makes for effective grouping. Churches, increasingly, are finding it advisable to group according to the public school grading, with boys and girls in the same classes.

g. Middle High Department, grades 9, 10 (ages 14, 15 approximately) has been created in some churches. Where this exists, the standards for Junior High and Senior High are adapted to the new department.

h. Senior High Department, grades 10, 11, 12 (ages 15, 16, 17 approximately). When the number exceeds twenty, it usually is wise to divide for classroom work.

i. Young Adult Department, ages 18 to 35 years. The practice of having a separate grouping for "older youth" has fallen into disfavor. In general the same principles would prevail for the Young Adult Department as for the Adult Department.

j. Adult Department, for those above 35 years of age. The number of members in an adult or young adult class will be conditioned by several factors, including teaching methods (discussion, lecture, etc.), available leadership, study materials, room size and location, and the nature of the group (men, women, or both). An ideal number in one situation may be unwise in another. To maintain person-to-person relationships and genuine fellowship within the group, adult classes should seldom exceed fifty persons in enrollment and should not exceed thirty to thirty-five in attendance. It is better to organize new groups than to increase numerically an existing group with new members who will have little opportunity to get acquainted or to exchange ideas. Whenever membership and space permit, a church should multiply the number of its adult classes. In this way, more people are apt to be reached for Christ.

k. The Home Department. This department brings the educational ministry of the church and the Sunday church school to adults who, through physical disability or necessary Sunday employment, are unable to participate regularly in the church worship and study sessions.

The school which is graded on the foregoing plan will require at least one teacher for each group. Where there is more than one class in an age group, the age group should be administered as a department with a departmental superintendent, secretary, and pianist in addition to the teachers.

The general superintendent is the executive in charge of the Sunday church school. All matters concerned with the effective functioning of the school, including those whose ultimate decision resides with the board of Christian education, should clear through the general superintendent. On the board of Christian education are committee chairmen in charge of children's work, youth work, and adult work. These persons will work closely with the age-group personnel in the various departments. In case of any serious difference of opinion between an age-group chairman and the Sunday church school superintendent, the board of Christian education is the arbiter. Ordinarily, however, such arbitration is not necessary, because all the board members as well as the superintendent are interested in a strong Christian teaching program for the church.

A Sunday church school of average size requires, in addition to the general superintendent and the departmental officers and teachers previously mentioned, one or more assistant superintendents, a secretary, and a treasurer.

The number of assistant superintendents depends upon the number of functions to be assigned to them. At least one assistant superintendent should be in training as a potential successor to the present superintendent. Whether or not the church is following the wise system of rotation in office through a mandatory limit on the number of successive years a person may serve in one office, it is always advisable that others be in training for responsible leadership.

Much of the secret of any superintendent's success lies in his intelligent distributing of responsibility. In a small school the superintendent and one assistant, together with the other members of his staff and the board of Christian education, can easily handle the varied activities of the school. But even so, the superintendent ought to let his assistant and other staff members grow through giving them increased responsibility. The test of the administrative ability of a superintendent in a school of any size is not his ability to do everything himself, but in getting others to use their talents in doing the work.

In a large school the superintendent may find value in having several assistants. One of these could be in charge of personnel. He would be responsible, therefore, for seeing that each department and class has a full staff of workers present each Sunday. He would keep the superintendent informed as to personnel needs.

Another assistant might be concerned with membership. He would have the twofold responsibility of maintaining regularity of attendance and of discovering ways of recruiting new pupils. He can find help in the programs of recruitment published by his denomination.

Yet another assistant might be in charge of special resources and equipment, such as audio-visual aids for use in the Sunday church school. Such an assistant would work closely with the board of Christian education and the committee on audio-visual aids.

One word of caution: the number of administrative personnel should be limited to those essential to the efficient functioning of the school. When administrative machinery becomes so complex that it takes more energy to keep it running than to do the job, it is time to simplify it.

THE SUNDAY CHURCH SCHOOL TIME SCHEDULE

In most churches the church school is held on Sunday morning, and it is related in schedule to the Sunday morning church service. In some churches, in an attempt to streamline the Sunday morning program, the school session and the morning worship service are combined. This should not be done in any way which leaves but little time for instruction. Several denominations are now developing plans to double the teaching time. Good teaching takes time, especially when methods of teaching are employed which are varied and effective.

In order to provide more time for the teaching of children, the Expanded Session plan has been adopted by many churches. Under this plan, in addition to the usual time allotted to the Sunday church school, a part or all of the church worship hour is used, thereby extending the period of learning activity for the children. Thus, instead of only one hour, the children have from one and one-half hours to two and one-half hours, making possible a varied program of graded worship and teaching. The denominational graded courses contain pages telling how to make the best use of this additional time.

The Unified Program of the church—if such a plan has been adopted—also affects the teaching program of the Sunday church school. Under this plan the church seeks to lead the children, youth, and adults of the church each Sunday

45

morning through a united experience of worship and study. Everyone is expected to share in this balanced program, thereby eliminating the practice of having some person come only to the "Sunday church school" and some only to "church." Because the duplication of worship and assembly programs is avoided in the youth and adult divisions, more time is available for study. The unified program usually uses the expanded session plan for the children.

A time schedule for a unified program—one frequently employed—is shown on the next page.

The Superintendent's Use of Records

Most superintendents are familiar with the graded and uniform lessons and the curriculum resources made available to the Sunday church schools. Some may not be so fully aware of the administrative helps also made available.

Records are of many types and serve various ends. No record should be kept, however, unless it fulfills a purpose that is clearly understood and considered important.

Attendance records have both group and individual values. The attendance within a department or in the whole school shows, over a period of time, whether or not the school is growing in the number of persons it is reaching. But records should also show the regularity of attendance for individual pupils and indicate those who have dropped out or been lost otherwise to the school. In addition, records will show class, departmental, and total school attendance. An analysis of these figures and a search for the reasons why certain classes or departments show more regularity of attendance than others will do much to reveal the points of strength and weakness within the school's program and teaching staff.

Most schools need more adequate records of each individual's progress within the educational program of the church and its school. Such a record would give the data

Nursery	Continuous Departmental Program 10:00 a.m.-12:15 p.m.	
Kindergarten	Continuous Departmental Program 10:00 a.m.-12:15 p.m.	
Primary	Church Worship Service 10:00-10:30 a.m.	Departmental Program 10:35 a.m.-12:15 p.m.
Junior	Church Worship Service 10:00-10:30 a.m.	Departmental Program 10:35 a.m.-12:15 p.m.
Junior High	Church Service 10:00-11:00 a.m.	Departmental Program 11:10 a.m.-12:15 p.m.
Senior High	Church Service 10:00-11:00 a.m.	Departmental Program 11:10 a.m.-12:15 p.m.
Young People	Church Service 10:00-11:00 a.m.	Departmental Program 11:10 a.m.-12:15 p.m.
Young Adult	Church Service 10:00-11:00 a.m.	Departmental Program 11:10 a.m.-12:15 p.m.
Adult	Church Service 10:00-11:00 a.m.	Departmental Program 11:10 a.m.-12:15 p.m.

when the pupil became a member of the school, his progress through the classes and departments, his regularity of attendance, special achievements, and personal development in leadership ability and experience.

Special records on the leadership of the school may also prove valuable. Such records indicate the courses of study taken by each officer and teacher, his regularity of attendance at workers' conferences, and other leadership information considered desirable.

The kind of financial records to be kept depends on the extent to which the Sunday church school has been integrated into the financial structure of the church as a whole. The financial records of a school which is a separate organization underwriting its own budget will be different from those of a school whose expenses are included in the budget of the church.

ENLISTING AND TRAINING TEACHERS

Leaders with different responsibilities are essential to the educational program of the Sunday church school. Of all the leaders, none is more needed than a good teacher. The small church with only a few classes is as much in need of good teachers as is the largest Sunday church school. Finding such teachers is one of the responsibilities of the board of Christian education. When choosing teachers, certain factors need to be borne in mind.

1. *Conviction:* The church must impress upon all its members that Christian education is important to its life, and that its program of Christian education, therefore, should be the finest possible. This conviction can be created and continuously strengthened through the pastor's sermons, through items in the church paper, through adequate equipment and financial support for the school's program, and through special ceremonies that keep Christian education and its workers prominent in the thinking of church members. Among the last named are installation services, the annual commissioning of officers and teachers, the annual banquet for Sunday church school workers, and the annual conference to plan the educational program of the church.

When the board of Christian education is considering the name of a prospective teacher, how should it proceed? (a) It should be sure, through careful investigation and consideration, that the person is the one wanted for that particular teaching opportunity. (b) It should choose carefully the right person to approach him with the invitation to teach. This may be a department superintendent, the pastor, the church director, the superintendent, or some member of the board of Christian education. It may seem wise to send two persons to extend the invitation to serve. Whoever is sent should be recognized as speaking for the board of Christian education and the church as a whole. (c) The representative of the board should arrange a personal conference in which he will have time to present adequately the challenge of the new responsibility. A casual call on the telephone or a quick urging during the rush between Sunday services may make the invitation seem trivial. Since teaching is important, one should not pretend that it is an easy task; the emphasis, rather, should be upon the great possibilities it affords to influence others for Christ and the conviction of the board of Christian education that the person approached is big enough for the job. (d) There may be those who sincerely doubt their ability to teach or lead. Such persons may begin their service as apprentice teachers or associate teachers.

The superintendent, or someone designated by him, should see that the work of the Sunday church school is constantly publicized. A continuous stream of news of specific educational undertakings and achievements provides better publicity than general statements to the effect that Christian education is important.

2. *Stewardship:* The church must develop among its members a sense of responsibility for the Christian stewardship of time and ability, as well as of money. New members, as they are welcomed into the church school, should be led to recognize this responsibility and make personal commitments in the light of it. The church, of course, is also responsible for distributing tasks and opportunities for service in such fashion that many persons can share in the work.

In addition to the basic policies that influence, consciously or otherwise, the procuring of teachers, there are certain procedures that can help in discovering prospective teachers: (a) The church membership roll should be studied and the possibilities of each member considered. (b) Teachers of older youth and adult classes should be asked to suggest the names of those within their classes who might make good teachers. (c) Within the women's society or the men's council, persons with potential or actual leadership ability will come to light. The superintendent should consider these persons in the light of the teaching needs of the school. (d) He should take note of those who are teaching in the local public schools or colleges. (e) A personal conference with each new church member will reveal prospective teachers. (f) Attempts should be made to enlist persons for service through individual conferences and through conferences with small groups or classes.

Teachers need training. They need to acquire information and to develop teaching skills; they need also inspiration and encouragement in their work. They usually feel the need for training in biblical knowledge. They need to be informed as to the psychological nature of the pupils they teach. Through training, a good teacher will become acquainted with the values inherent in various methods of teaching, particularly those suited for use with his class. Any teacher will benefit personally and will be a better teacher if he has discovered the relationship of his class to the total program of the church. Training will help a teacher to understand the various areas of curriculum interest and their meaning for the persons he teaches.

Leadership education may be classified as formal and informal. Formal leadership education refers to specific courses of study carried on under supervision. Such courses are listed as part of the Leadership Education Curriculum promoted by the National Council of the Churches of Christ in the U.S.A. and by the constituent denominations. They include general courses on the Bible, personal Christian living, the psychology of pupils, and methods of teaching. There are specialized courses for workers with children, with youth, and with adults, as well as for superintendents and others who must carry administrative responsibilities.

Informal leadership training refers to (a) apprentice teaching, (b) practice teaching under supervision, (c) observing other teachers, (d) monthly workers' conferences, (e) conferences with workers from other Sunday church schools at community, state, or national gatherings, (f) guided reading of books and magazines.

The Certificate of Progress is a worthy method of recognizing a person's progress in a balanced program of training through personal religious development, churchmanship, and educational growth. There are three types of certificates of progress; namely, First, Second, and Third. The requirements for the Second Certificate of Progress, for example, are listed below:

RELIGIOUS DEVELOPMENT

1. The use of a plan of personal devotional practices covering a period of two years—reading the Bible, prayer, church participation.

CHURCHMANSHIP

2. Participation in the worship, fellowship, and financial support of the church.

3. Two years of experience in church work or as a leader in a community activity approved by the church.

EDUCATIONAL GROWTH

4. Reading: (a) Regularly, a Christian education magazine, (b) two or more recent books on Christian education.

5. Meetings: Attendance at workers' conferences, institutes, conventions, assemblies, over a period of two years.

6. Study Courses: With respect to courses, the student is required to complete six Second Series courses, or twelve First Series courses, or an equivalent combination, which may include those completed for a First Certificate of Progress. These courses should be distributed as follows: four Second Series courses selected from Group I or the equivalent of similar First Series courses; two from the student's

special field of work to be selected from Groups II to VII or the equivalent of similar courses from the First Series.[1]

Genuine growth in Christian leadership comes, of course, not merely from training, but primarily from a deep sense of one's Christian stewardship of time and ability, coupled with a willingness to undertake tasks that may seem to be beyond one's powers. Such a willingness is nurtured and stimulated through the faith that one is working with God. Basic to any training, therefore, must be the daily practice of prayer, devotional reading, and meditation. The pressure of accumulating tasks must never be permitted to crowd these practices from the daily schedule of the Christian worker.

QUESTIONS AND PROJECTS

1. Assuming that the board of Christian education has responsibility for enlisting and training workers, discuss the personnel who would select the following: (a) a primary teacher for a Sunday church school, (b) the superintendent of the Junior High Department, (c) the general superintendent, (d) the pianist in the adult department.

2. Discuss the most helpful ways to train your workers.

3. Be prepared to explain to the group how your Sunday church school is organized.

4. Discuss the use made of the records kept by your Sunday church school.

5. Prepare a time schedule for the various departments, or for a one-room school. Indicate the time you think should be given to each of the following: (a) worship, (b) the class session, (c) the taking of records, (d) fellowship, (e) other items.

6. During the next two Sundays carry out the following

[1] For complete information the superintendent should write to the Leadership Education Department of his denomination, at either its local (state) or national headquarters.

survey in all departments (or, at least, in one department of the children's division, one department of the youth division, and one department of the adult division) of your Sunday church school: (a) record the time each group began, (b) how many teachers and officers were on time or present in advance of the time scheduled for opening, (c) how many teachers and officers were late, (d) how many of your teachers and officers were absent without adequate preparation being made by other persons to take over their work.

Chapter 4

THE GENERAL SUPERINTENDENT
WORKS WITH OTHERS

As THE GENERAL SUPERINTENDENT goes about his work, he will find that many people contribute to the effectiveness of his administrative leadership. In fact, not only the satisfaction he finds in his task, but also the morale of the school will be affected greatly by those with whom he is associated. His working relationships with them, therefore, are important. Through them the work of the school gets done; through them the Christian teaching program of the school achieves its goals.

CHURCH SCHOOL PERSONNEL

1. *The Pupils:* In one sense, the superintendent works with all the members of the Sunday church school classes. But many of his relationships with them are indirect; that is, through the teachers and administrative staff. Yet in the course of a year he will on many occasions be in direct personal contact with the pupils. To them he is the symbol of the organization of which he is superintendent. Such identification brings opportunities as well as responsibilities. Through these contacts he may bring additional workers to his side. The youth who today admires the superintendent and the spirit in which he does his work, may be inspired, ten years from now, to accept the same honor and responsibility. Any superintendent with a long-term concern for the growth and improvement of his school will not neglect his relationships with the pupils—children and youth, as well as adults.

```
┌─────────────────────────────────────────┐
│                                           │
│         THE SUPERINTENDENT                │
│                                           │
│              works with                   │
│                                           │
│               PUPILS                      │
│              TEACHERS                     │
│              MINISTER                     │
│   DIRECTOR OF CHRISTIAN EDUCATION         │
│    BOARD OF CHRISTIAN EDUCATION           │
│               CHURCH                      │
│             COMMUNITY                     │
│      HIS ADMINISTRATIVE STAFF             │
│                                           │
└─────────────────────────────────────────┘
```

2. *The Teachers:* No matter how large or small a school may be, teachers are essential members of the Sunday church school staff, and with them the superintendent must work. If teachers enjoy their work, if they have the equipment they need, if they are encouraged in their search for added training, and if they feel that their achievements are sincerely appreciated and recognized, they will produce amazing results with their pupils.

The superintendent of a small school usually is in close contact with his teachers. Together they work and plan in order that their school may grow and improve its program. In a larger school, the normal channels of communication between the general superintendent and the teachers are through the departmental superintendents. But whatever the size of the school, the relationship between the superintendent and the teachers is of vital importance.

The devotion which the superintendent gives to his task becomes an inspiration to the teachers. If they feel that he has a genuine appreciation of the importance of his responsibility, they will respond more readily to his challenge to them to do their work well. The authority of the superintendent is most effectively wielded through encouragement, persuasion, and the power of example. The teachers do their work for the same reasons that he does his: loyalty to Christ and his church, genuine interest in persons, and a conviction that the teaching ministry of the church is important. The superintendent's leadership will be successful, therefore, not to the extent that he may seek to "throw his weight around," but to the extent that he can persuade his co-workers that the suggestions he makes will bring improvement to the Sunday church school.

The superintendent, as an ex-officio member of the board of Christian education, has a voice in the choice of teachers, but his relationship to them does not stop there. He should help his teachers through his personal comments and guidance to recognize and appreciate the significance of their opportunities. He should encourage each teacher to increase his skill in leadership through recommended reading and study, through participation in conferences, and through attendance at training classes. He should show an understanding of each teacher's work, commenting with approval upon noteworthy achievements and calling attention to possible changes that will make for improvement. Growth through Christian training and experience should be as real for teachers as for pupils. The superintendent can help to make it so.

3. *The Minister:* The minister is the executive leader of the church as a whole, as the superintendent is the executive leader of the Sunday church school, a part of that whole.

Other relationships, of course, exist between them: the minister is the pastor of the church and the superintendent is one of the members; the minister is the worship leader and preacher, and the superintendent is a member of the congregation; and, finally, the superintendent is a member of the church fellowship which called the minister to be its pastor, preacher, and administrator.

Technically, the superintendent is the executive of one phase of the church life, and he works with the pastor, the chief administrator. In actual practice, however, most pastors and their church school superintendents seek to work as a team because of their mutual concern for the welfare of the church and its teaching program, and because they respect each other's motives and hopes for the church. Even when differences of opinion may appear on specific issues, if there is a basic respect for each other, such differences can be resolved. Patience, prayer, and mutual regard can do much where pastor and superintendent recognize and appreciate the devotion and integrity of each other.

The pastor and superintendent will not decide policy changes in the functioning of the school. Those are matters for the board of Christian education to work out. As ex-officio members of the board, however, both pastor and superintendent have the opportunity to suggest in board meetings such policy changes as they may consider advisable. They likewise share in the decisions of the board.

There are many practical details in the work of the school in which the superintendent and the pastor can be of help to each other. The superintendent will find it helpful to draw on the pastor's experience in previous situations, or he may find in their mutual explorations of various possibilities that answers can be worked out together that neither could have reached separately.

The church and its Sunday church school have a responsibility for ministering to the same persons. The superintendent and the pastor, working together, can do much to give the teaching program a significant place in the total life of the church. This will assist the board to enlist top-quality personnel for its leadership and to provide adequate teaching materials, equipment, and space. With pastor and superintendent working as a team, both are enriched through the relationship. Technically, of course, decisions officially guiding the superintendent in his work are made by the board of Christian education, not by the superintendent and pastor working apart from the board. The finest values in the superintendent-pastor relationship lie not so much in official directives as in the mutual sharing of a common responsibility for the spiritual nurture of children, youth, and adults.

4. *The Director of Christian Education:* If a church has a director of Christian education, the relationship between the superintendent and the director is similar to that existing between the superintendent and the pastor. It is expected, of course, that the director will be a person thoroughly trained in the field of Christian education, and one competent, therefore, not only to direct the total educational program of the church, but also to give expert guidance to those who work with him (or her), such as the superintendent of the Sunday church school and the counselors of the youth groups.

The basic policies of the church in regard to its educational program are determined by the board of Christian education. What then, are the relationships of the board, the director of Christian education, and the superintendent of the Sunday church school to the various phases of the church's educational program? Let us use the area of leadership education as an illustration. The board member responsible for an effective church program of leadership education will find the director of real value in terms of guidance and administration. In setting up or directing such a program, the superintendent, on his part, will point out the leadership needs of the school and tell what he hopes may be accomplished by the program.

Again, the director of Christian education will guide and assist the personnel committee of the board in discovering and enlisting persons for the various tasks connected with the educational program of the church. The superintendent, on his part, will make known to the board the leadership personnel needs of the Sunday church school. As a member of the board, the superintendent will have a voice in the selection and approval of the persons chosen as workers.

This, in general, defines the respective fields of service filled by the superintendent and the director of Christian education. In a specific situation, these relationships should be worked out to the best advantage of the teaching program of the church.

5. *The Board of Christian Education:* The board of Christian education is the board to which the superintendent is directly responsible. Whether elected by the church or appointed by the board, the superintendent reports regularly to the board and brings to its attention the needs as well as the achievements of the school.

The superintendent will find that the board gives much of its time, thought, and effort to the Sunday church school. Because of his executive relationship to the school, his analysis of its needs and his suggestions for meeting them will carry considerable weight with the board. He will discover that the more closely he co-operates with the board, the more effective his leadership will become.

The superintendent, by virtue of his intimate knowledge of the Sunday church school, will be able to make a significant contribution to the work of the board, particularly as it relates to the Sunday church school. At the same time, through his connection with the board, the superintendent will gain a greater appreciation of the total education program of the church and of the relationship between the

Sunday church school and the other phases of the church's educational work. The Youth Fellowship Sunday morning and evening unified program, for example, and its relationship to the Sunday church school will be better understood and better co-ordinated by the superintendent as he functions as a member of the board of Christian education.

The age-group committees of the board of Christian education will work closely with the superintendent of the school as they give consideration to the special needs of the specific age divisions for which they are responsible. Such age-group committees do not function in executive or administrative capacity within the Sunday church school. Their findings and suggestions are brought to the board for consideration as it fashions the policies and makes the decisions that guide the superintendent in his executive responsibility. Such committees can be a source of much practical help.

The church school librarian usually serves under the jurisdiction of the board of Christian education, possibly as a member of the Committee on Leadership Education. Again, however, the superintendent will find that the library and its librarian can be helpful in furnishing his workers on a loan basis with books and magazines which will stimulate their development and increase their ability. The superintendent will be wise to emphasize the values of the library both in his contacts with his workers and in the board meetings where budgetary matters are determined. A good library, constantly used, can be a big asset to the Sunday church school.

6. *Church and Community Relationships:* As the official head of the Sunday church school, the superintendent will have occasion from time to time to represent the school in its participation in other church activities, as well as in interchurch activities in the community. At times such extra responsibilities may seem burdensome, but he, by participating, can make an important contribution to the morale of the

chool. If there is any question in his own mind as to the
isdom of his participation in a specific event or project
s official representative of the Sunday church school, he
ill find it helpful to turn to the board of Christian educa-
on for counsel.

7. *The Superintendent's Staff:* The number of those who
nake up the staff of the Sunday church school will vary
ith the size of the school. A school with an attendance
nder seventy-five will probably have a staff of several
eachers, a secretary, a treasurer, and possibly an assistant
uperintendent. A larger school may well add not only addi-
ional teachers, but also departmental or divisional superin-
endents, departmental secretaries, an additional secretary
or the church school, and possibly another assistant super-
ntendent.

The larger the school, the more indirect becomes the rela-
ionship between the general superintendent and the teachers.
et, as indicated earlier, that relationship is important; and
he superintendent should do all in his power to maintain the
norale of the teachers through his relationships with them,
hrough his public references to them, and through the appre-
iation he expresses for their work from time to time.

In a larger school, the superintendent will work closely
ith the departmental or divisional superintendents. Schools
ith two or more classes within a departmental classifica-
ion (Nursery, Kindergarten, Primary, etc.) are usually
rganized into departmental units of several classes, with a
epartmental superintendent in charge of each unit. In some
chools, the organization may be on the basis of a children's
ivision, a youth division, and an adult division.

Such departmental or divisional superintendents give con-
tant supervision to the work of their teachers and classes,
ossibly leading or planning worship, noting curriculum
naterials and resources needed, and keeping the general
uperintendent informed as to the basic program and the

possibilities of improving it. Such persons are part of th superintendent's executive staff. Because of their close rela tionship to the teachers and pupils, their observations an suggestions are significant. The alert superintendent wi profit by them. Although technically the departmental supe intendents are subordinate to the general superintendent, h will build a finer school, with a more wholesome morale if he treats them as partners rather than as subordinates. H can learn much, if he will, from his departmental leader

The secretary, or secretaries, in most schools, have thre major responsibilities: (a) correspondence, (b) record keep ing, and (c) ordering and distributing supplies. In a sma. school these responsibilities may be handled by one person In a very large school, a general secretary with three assis ants may discharge these duties. In the average school, on secretary handles correspondence and orders supplies, an the other keeps the records of the school.

The Sunday church school superintendent will find th work of the secretary, or secretaries, of much help in th smooth and efficient functioning of the school. Records ar important, although the answer to the question of *how im portant* depends in large measure on the relevance of th records to the work of the school. It is sound policy t examine and evaluate periodically the method of recor keeping and the type of information recorded. Some recor keeping may be found to be a compiling of facts used b no one. On the other hand, information may be needed tha is not now being recorded.

The ordering and distributing of supplies have an impor tant bearing on the morale of the school. Inadequate o insufficient materials create within the teaching staff a feel ing of non-support. Supplies that arrive late, due to dela in ordering, produce irritation, or ultimately, indifference.

The above reasons make clear the importance of the worl done by the secretaries. The superintendent, therefore

hould recognize those secretaries whose work is noteworthy and give guidance to those who need suggestions
or improvement.

The treasurer needs to be accurate as well as honest.
romptness in the payment of bills, care in charging ex-
enses to appropriate budgetary items, accuracy in keeping
nancial records—all these make a good treasurer a joy to
ave in the administration of the school. The requirements
re few, but absolutely necessary. A wise superintendent will
ive thanks for a good treasurer and will recognize in him
 valuable co-worker.

Every superintendent should have one or more assistants.
ven in a small school, the superintendent will do well to
ave an assistant, if for no other reason than to train him
or future responsibility. In a small school, the superintend-
nt will probably have the assistant share in a variety of
esponsibilities so as to give him thorough training in many
ifferent phases of the work.

In a larger school, assistants are sometimes assigned spe-
ialized responsibilities under the supervision of the general
uperintendent. One assistant, for example, may be con-
erned with membership. His duty involves not only the
vinning of new members, but also the retention of those
lready enrolled. Such a person should study the records
f those attending infrequently as over against those who
ome regularly. He should then seek to find the reasons for
he irregular attendance, thus helping to emphasize the
mportance of individual frequency of attendance and of
ncreased enrollment.

Another assistant may be assigned the responsibility of
urchasing and improving equipment. This would involve
nore than the routine reporting of needed supplies or equip-
nent by teachers or departmental superintendents. It would
equire a study of new resources, such as those in the audio-
risual field, and an analysis of their worth and suitability

to the school in the light of its Christian teaching goals and procedures.

Such assistants would work in close co-operation with the general superintendent and would report to him their findings and suggestions. He, in turn, would relay them to the board of Christian education for due consideration.

In this chapter we have sought to indicate the significant personal relationships of the general superintendent in his leadership of the Sunday church school. Obviously, in all such relationships, the general suggestions that have been made will be complicated or strengthened by the personality, qualities, and attitudes of each person involved. Under such circumstances, however, the superintendent will find it helpful to read and digest 1 Corinthians 13:4-7. One of the modern translations may be helpful.

QUESTIONS AND PROJECTS

1. Discuss the statement: "The superintendent is a symbol of the Sunday church school."

2. What is the relationship of the superintendent to the pastor? to the church director of Christian education? to the general secretary, the assistant superintendent, and the other officers?

3. Write a paragraph on how a good superintendent co-operates with the board of Christian education. Suggest ways by which the board can make the work of the superintendent easier.

Chapter 5

THE WORKERS' CONFERENCE

THE WORKERS' CONFERENCE provides the occasion when the church school workers confer concerning their work: its purpose, its achievements, its failures, and the use of more effective ways of achieving its goals and objectives.

The church school superintendent should know that every moment spent in planning a worth-while workers' conference and in enlisting the 100 per cent attendance of his workers is time well spent. It makes for a stronger school by achieving several objectives:

VALUES OF THE WORKERS' CONFERENCE

1. *Recognition:* When a Sunday church school worker is properly recruited, he is impressed with the fact that he

---

A WORKERS' CONFERENCE

provides

RECOGNITION

FELLOWSHIP

IMPROVEMENT

INSPIRATION

PLANNING

---

is making a contribution to a significant expression of the church's life—its Christian teaching program. The workers' conference emphasizes the importance of that teaching program and the workers' contribution to it. Furthermore, as the various phases of the school's program come under consideration, the achievements of the successful workers will be noted by their colleagues. Valid recognition of individual as well as group achievement constitutes one value of the workers' conference.

2. *Fellowship:* True fellowship grows out of a genuine concern for the shared interest or mutual responsibility. The church school worker shares with his co-workers a concern for the success of his efforts and, consciously or unconsciously, for the success of the school as a whole. He needs, therefore, fellowship with his co-workers from time to time, especially since much of his work must be done separately from them.

Whereas the teacher of a class, for example, participates in the fellowship of his class, he works alone so far as his co-workers in the school are concerned. Casual meetings of fellow-teachers and the momentary exploration of their experiences serve only to accentuate the basic lack of more frequent fellowship in their common responsibilities. Only the regular scheduling of workers' conferences insures frequent occasions for the fellowship so vital to the continuing morale of the school's workers.

3. *Improvement:* The workers' conferences can be of help both in stimulating the desire for improvement and in showing the way by which it can be achieved. Where the school is large enough, departmental conferences will be concerned with practical ways in which such improvement can be made within the several departments. But individual improvement, as well as that of the school as a whole, should be a major concern of the general workers' conference. The workers'

conference program for the ensuing year, therefore, should be so planned as to provide specific elements leading to the improvement of the school and of the individual teachers and officers. This may mean either that a portion of the program will be given over to a leadership training course or that there will be a series of sessions concerned with those phases of the school's program which stand in the greatest need of improvement. Some suggestions for this purpose will be offered later in this chapter.

4. *Inspiration:* A successful workers' conference will send out its workers inspired to do better work—not merely with a recognition that better work should be done or with only an understanding of how it might be done. There needs to be a strong conviction that the work can and must be done, and that there is joy to be found in the doing of it. Occasionally an outside speaker may bring an inspirational message; more frequently, however, the stimulus should come from the nature and atmosphere of the workers' conference itself. If the program elements seem truly relevant to the workers, and if they open vistas of new and better approaches to their tasks, the conference will serve to bring enduring inspiration to the workers.

The worship phase of the program ought to bring spiritual uplift, for in it emphasis may be placed on the fact that we are not only workers, and workers together, but also workers together with God.

5. *Planning:* The workers' conference can waste much time dealing with administrative details that lie in the hands of the board of Christian education or of some executive officer of the Sunday church school. Actually, where there is a properly functioning board of Christian education and a capable superintendent with his executive associates, there is no need to spend its time on administrative matters.

It must be said, however, that there are administrative concerns, policies, and decisions that directly affect the workers. Such matters merit discussion, understanding, and evaluation by the workers, particularly where the success of such policies and decisions depends in large measure upon their full co-operation.

Although decisions as to curriculum, grading, space, and time schedules are to be made by the board of Christian education, all these matters should be adequately interpreted to the workers and discussed by them. Such matters should be carefully outlined and factually supported before being brought up for consideration. Routine matters of business, however, should not be permitted to take up the time allotted for the program. If the workers are to understand the objectives of the school and if they are to work together to achieve them, they should have opportunity to share in the planning. Out of such discussion and planning will come an awareness of the problem areas that need more thorough consideration. These may become subjects for systematic study by the group at a later time.

HELPFUL PROCEDURES

An effective workers' conference depends on adequate planning and preparation. The superintendent of the Sunday church school, as the executive leader of the school, is responsible for the success of these meetings. This does not mean that he alone prepares and conducts the programs. But it does mean that he, as leader of the school, cannot afford to have weak or ineffective workers' conferences.

1. *Organization:* The superintendent, or someone he designates, should preside at the workers' conferences. In planning for the conferences, he will work with a program committee. This committee will consist of the general superintendent, the chairman of leadership education for the church, and representatives of the department superintendents and teachers in the children's, youth, and adult divisions of the Sunday church school.

2. *Attendance:* The workers' conference should strive for 100 per cent attendance of those persons serving in the school. Included are the teachers, the department superintendents, the divisional superintendents (chairmen of children's, youth, and adult work), the treasurer, the librarian, the secretaries, the assistant superintendents, the general superintendent, the director of Christian, education, and the pastor.

How often should the workers' conference meet? Through experimentation and experience it has been found valuable to have the conferences once a month throughout the entire year. Although some churches discontinue the workers' conferences in the summer, other churches have capitalized on this period for review of the previous year's work and for planning the work for the year to come. It is well to establish a definite night each month, such as the second Tuesday. Thus each worker can reserve the date and keep it free of conflicts.

Where should the workers' conference be held? Occasionally it may seem wise, because of local conditions or the size of the group, to hold the meeting in a home. Such a setting usually adds much to the feeling of fellowship. Unless care is exercised, however, the fellowship may profit at the expense of constructive work.

Most workers' conferences are held in the church. It is important to choose a room that is adequate but not too large. A group lost in a large room is apt to feel equally lost in its search for fellowship with one another. On the other hand, a group cramped in a little room may well react in an unconscious or conscious irritation that will color the proceedings adversely. The superintendent, therefore, will do well to see that the room is adequate in size, properly ventilated, neat, clean, and well lighted. These seemingly trivial matters will do much toward the success of the conference.

3. *Planning the Program:* The program involves, in addition to the physical setting, three basic elements: program content, time schedule, and leadership. These call for separate consideration.

The program content is organized usually about four factors, of which worship is the first. Do not let this potentially significant experience deteriorate into dullness through a monotonous repetition of the same worship pattern. Worship leadership, with creative concern for its worth, can do much to bring a spiritual dimension to the whole workers' conference. Excellent suggestions for worship can be found in denominational magazines and in other worship resource materials.

Policies, problems, needs, and opportunities peculiar to the school itself constitute the second factor. Time should be provided for considering the decisions of the board of Christian education as they affect the work of the Sunday church school. Matters on which the judgment of the workers is needed before decisions are reached, should be brought up at this point. Workers should have an opportunity to offer suggestions for the improvement of the school. When crucial decisions are to be made, it is important to have the supporting facts and the opposing facts ready for presentation. In addition, when decisions have been made, the appropriate person or group responsible for carrying out the decision should be made aware of the assignment.

The third factor in the program content is what may be called the "program feature." This may be a leadership training session, a thorough consideration of a major policy change, a session for reviewing and planning, or a guest speaker. Suggestions for this phase of the workers' conference program will be offered later in this chapter.

The departmental planning period is usually the fourth factor in the program content. Many matters are of concern only to a single department. Time, therefore, should be allowed for departmental conferences during which the teachers and departmental superintendents can confer about the situation within their departments. In some churches, the time schedule of the workers' conference immediately preceding a new quarter's teaching program is adjusted so as to allow more time for departmental planning. In other churches, an additional departmental planning session is held in September, December, March, and June to prepare for the ensuing quarter. In a small school, where separate departments are not practical, divisional (children's, youth, and adult) planning conferences can be of help in meeting the problems and opportunities peculiar to each age group.

4. *Determining the Time Schedule:* The time schedule for the workers' conference can be arranged in any one of several ways. If, for example, a leadership training course is to be the program feature for a series of six workers' conferences, fifty minutes should be allowed for it. For other program features, thirty to forty minutes may be sufficient.

Various time schedules are suggested below.

Schedule A

7:30 p.m.	Worship
7:40 p.m.	Program feature
8:10 p.m.	School policies and needs discussed
8:30 p.m.	Departmental conferences
9:30 p.m.	Adjournment

Schedule B

7:15 p.m.	Departmental conferences
8:20 p.m.	Recess
8:30 p.m.	Worship
8:40 p.m.	Program feature
9:10 p.m.	School policies and needs discussed
9:30 p.m.	Adjournment

Schedule C

7:15 p.m.	Leadership training course
8:10 p.m.	Worship
8:20 p.m.	School policies and needs discussed
8:45 p.m.	Departmental conferences
9:30 p.m.	Adjournment

Schedule D

7:30 p.m.	Worship
7:40 p.m.	Program feature
8:45 p.m.	School policies and needs discussed
9:00 p.m.	Fellowship and refreshments
9:30 p.m.	Adjournment

The above schedules, of course, are merely suggestions. There may be occasions when some major change in school policy will make it wise to combine the time usually devoted to a program feature with that reserved for the discussion of policies and needs, thereby making available a full hour or more of time.

Many churches have experimented successfully with a workers' conference that includes a dinner. They feel that eating together does much for the experience of fellowship within the group. The dinner also enables the conference sessions to begin earlier in the evening.

Schedule E

6:00 p.m.	Dinner
6:50 p.m.	Worship
7:00 p.m.	School policies and needs discussed
7:20 p.m.	Program feature or leadership class
8:15 p.m.	Departmental conferences
9:15 p.m.	Adjournment

Schedule F

6:00 p.m.	Dinner
6:50 p.m.	Program feature or leadership class

7:40 p.m.	Worship
7:50 p.m.	School policies and needs discussed
8:15 p.m.	Departmental conferences
9:15 p.m.	Adjournment

SCHEDULE G

6:00 p.m.	Dinner
6:40 p.m.	School policies and needs discussed
7:00 p.m.	Recess
7:15 p.m.	Worship
7:45 p.m.	Program feature
8:15 p.m.	Departmental conferences
9:00 p.m.	Adjournment

SCHEDULE H

6:30 p.m.	Dinner
7:20 p.m.	Worship
7:30 p.m.	Program feature
8:40 p.m.	School policies and needs discussed
9:00 p.m.	Adjournment

The four factors in a complete workers' conference session are worship, departmental conferences, discussion of current school policies and needs, and the program feature.

PLANNING THE PROGRAM

1. *The Worship Period:* An abundance of worship suggestions can be found in the religious educational magazines, denominational and interdenominational, and in the many books of devotions, which are available. The theme of the worship service should be related to the program feature for the evening.

2. *The Departmental Conferences:* In them the time frequently is devoted to planning for the units next to be taught, together with the consideration of matters of special importance to their departments. When conclusions are reached which concern the entire school, they should be shared with the appropriate personnel for further consideration and

PROGRAM FACTORS

are

WORSHIP

DEPARTMENTAL PLANNING

DISCUSSION: POLICIES AND NEEDS

PROGRAM FEATURE

action. Department superintendents who are in charge of this part of the program will need to plan carefully in order that the time shall be used profitably.

3. *Policies and Needs:* The discussion of current school policies and needs grows out of (1) recommendations from the board of Christian education, (2) special days and occasions in the church school, (3) suggestions from the school staff itself. A detailed agenda should be planned prior to the meeting, and the information needed for intelligent and profitable discussion should be available. It will be helpful to inform the workers ahead of time as to the matters to be considered.

The above three factors find their variety in content growing out of the changing conditions of the school and the seasons of the year. The program feature, however, will make its best contribution if it is planned as part of a sequence over a series of meetings. This is preferable to a last minute search for something interesting to add to the conference program.

4. *The Program Feature:* This, as well as the other program factors, should grow out of the needs, opportunities,

and problems of the workers. Although occasionally it may seem wise to have a speaker from the outside because of a special contribution he or she can make, usually it is wiser to make use of the workers themselves in developing the program feature. They are acquainted with the needs that must be met, and they will profit personally by the work they do in preparation for the conference. Good judgment should be used, however, in making assignments in order that the program will be both interesting and helpful.

Many resources are available to help those responsible for this phase of the workers' conference program. For example, one denomination prepares each year a series of twelve workers' conference programs. Detailed suggestions and resources for each program appear in the denominational teachers' magazine for the month prior to the conference in which the theme is to be used. Some annual themes in recent years have been:

Creative Methods in Christian Teaching
The Christian Teacher and the Bible
The Worshiping Church

The twelve programs under Creative Methods in Christian Teaching include the following interesting suggestions for meetings from September through August:

Methods — A Means to Creative Teaching
Team Teaching
The Art of Group Conversation
Teaching-Learning Experiences
Session Purpose Determines Methods
Use of the Dialogical
Planning the Class Session
The Teacher's Role in Discussion
The Home Shares in the Teaching Process
Creative Use of Audio-Visuals
The Role of the Teacher in Role-Playing
We Take Account of Our Work

After such a series, all of the workers will have a deepened appreciation of the place of the Bible in Christian teaching, and they will be better equipped to use the Bible intelligently.

You will note that eleven of the twelve workers' conferences are specially related to the year's special theme. Whatever the annual theme for the program feature in the workers' conference may be, it is considered advisable to devote a session to review and planning. When summer comes, it is well to review the achievements and failures of the past year, and to plan the principal objectives for the year to come. This session is followed by one devoted to the consideration of special ways by which the coming year's objectives will be attained. Finally, if and when local conditions warrant, a picnic of some kind may take the place of the year's final workers' conference.

The themes for the program feature are almost unlimited. For example, there is the whole field of leadership training courses sponsored by the leadership education department of your denomination. Choose one that your workers feel will be especially helpful to them. A first series course might well be used for a six-months' period, releasing the other six months for other types of programs.

Another series of programs might be organized around the goals for an effective Sunday church school.

Finally, the workers themselves may be asked to indicate the fields in which they feel the greatest need of help. The program committee of the workers' conference could then take these suggestions and plan a year's series around them. In so doing, they should utilize resource books, magazines, and such audio-visual aids as the filmstrip "Together We Grow" (on the Workers Conference) and "A Mirror to Myself" (on supervision)—from the Church School Administration Audio-Visual Kit.[1]

[1] Prepared by the National Council of Church of Christ in the U.S.A.

The workers' conference is the power-center for an effec-
ve Sunday church school staff. Get every worker to attend;
en guide them by means of an interesting and helpful
ogram that will make them glad they came.

QUESTIONS AND PROJECTS

1. What are the values of holding workers' conferences?
st on a sheet of paper several such values.

2. Who should plan the workers' conference programs?

3. About how much time is spent on the various phases
the workers' conference programs held in your church,
ch as the worship, business, and main feature? What
anges in the time schedule do you believe would benefit
ur programs?

4. Suggest a theme for a year's workers' conference pro-
ams for your Sunday church school and list possible
onthly titles.

5. Build a detailed program for a monthly workers' con-
rence, including the time schedule.

Chapter 6

THE SPIRITUAL LIFE OF THE
SUNDAY CHURCH SCHOOL

IF THE SUPERINTENDENT is to guide the school in ¡ emphasis on the reality of the presence and power God in life, that experience must be real in his own life. superintendent may make errors in administrative judgme and yet, because of the genuineness of his dedication a devotion to his work, be the leader of a growing and effe tive school. On the other hand, excellence of organization structure cannot make amends for spiritual insincerity apathy.

THE SUPERINTENDENT AND THE SPIRITUAL LIFE
OF THE SCHOOL

A dedicated Christian layman, who has served as supe intendent of one of the largest Sunday church schools our nation, expressed his conviction that the superintende needs to have a program for promoting his own spiritu growth. "People who find satisfaction in exercising the administrative talents," he said, "sometimes do so to t neglect of the contemplative side of their lives. They m need to put forth special effort to insure that their ow Christian experiences become increasingly significant." O basic way, then, by which the superintendent may influen the spiritual life of the Sunday church school is through t reality of his own growing spiritual life.

In the second place, the superintendent will keep co stantly before his workers, as well as before the entire chur constituency, the school's emphasis upon Christian commi ment and growth in Christian character and influence. Th

: will do not only in the workers' conferences, but also ɔm time to time on informal occasions and in public meetgs. If the denomination has one over-all objective in Chris-ιn education, it should be adopted as the stated objective the church school. He should make it familiar to the hole church, as well as to the church school leaders. In lition to publishing it in the church bulletin for Christian lucation Week, reference should be made to it frequently ɾoughout the year. It should serve as a standard by which ggestions for changes in the Sunday church school cur-ɪulum or practices may be judged. In addition, it will ·lp to make clear that the basic objective of the Sunday urch school is really the basic objective of the total church llowship.

In the third place, the superintendent who would empha-ɀe the essential spiritual purpose of the Sunday church hool can accomplish much by encouraging the departmental perintendents, and other workers responsible for worship, recognize the value of graded worship and its central ɡnificance for the whole program of Christian education. ɾue worship grows out of reactions to experiences. Wor-ɪip which is related to, or grows out of, other Christian lucational experiences is capable of being made the best nd of worship. The departmental superintendent or other orship leader should be alert to these opportunities.

Whenever the superintendent himself is in charge of a ɔrship service, he can strengthen the spiritual realities in ιe life of the members of his school by his careful per-ʌnal preparation of that service and by his reverent attitude hen leading it. In these ways he reveals his appreciation ʹ its importance. The casual or hasty last minute search ·r hymns or the stumbling reading of an ill-digested Scrip-ɾe passage not only drains the life out of the worship ɾvice, but also proclaims in unmistakable terms that in his ɕimation worship is merely a trivial tradition of empty value. On the other hand, a thoughtfully prepared service led in reverent spirit, can make worship a memorable moment in the spiritual growth of everyone participating.

The superintendent will find it a profitable experience not only for himself but also for the school, to make a study of worship: its nature, its rich resources, and its many possible variations. The results of this study will be helpful on those occasions when he is personally responsible for leading worship; they will also be of service when he is called on to train others in the preparation and leadership of worship services.

Finally, the superintendent can influence the spiritual life of the Sunday church school through building up that section of the church library that deals with worship, including its department of audio-visual aids. New teachers should be introduced to the library and encouraged to make use of it. The superintendent may find it helpful to enlist some person to become a resource person in worship, ready to assist other church school leaders in discovering more effective ways of guiding the worship of their groups.

THE WORSHIP SERVICES OF THE SCHOOL

1. *In the Small Church:* In most of our one-room churches the Sunday church school worship service is usually at a fixed time with all ages participating. Sometimes it comes as part of an assembly period in which announcements and matters of business may be included. Despite the limitations that this wide age-span places on the use of worship resources there are certain things that can be done to make the worship service during the assembly period more valuable spiritually to those participating.

In planning the service, recognition should be given to the presence of the children. If the service is planned so that its various parts are meaningful to them, everyone will benefit by the service; whereas, if the service is planned for

80

adults only, it will have little constructive value for children and youth. The Bible passages, hymns, prayers, and interpretation, should all be selected not only because of their appropriateness to the worship theme, but also because of their worth for all ages.

In a one-room school, the superintendent might assign to individuals of the various age-groups parts of the worship service, so that many may receive experience in conducting worship. Also, occasionally, a class might be asked to plan and conduct the worship service.

In arranging a worship center, pictures serve well. If from time to time the picture displayed as expressive of the worship theme is chosen from the picture sets used in the children's classes, this will indicate that the younger participants in the service are being considered.

Music, pictures, and stories will enrich and add variety to the worship. The superintendent, when planning a worship service, will find useful the general suggestions given later in this chapter in the section entitled, "Elements of Worship." In the assembly period matters of business and announcements should be eliminated or kept to a minimum. This will improve the possibilities of a worship experience and also allow more time for the class session.

Every child and youth, if at all possible, should have the privilege of participating in graded worship. This may not always be practical in a one-room church building. If two or more additional rooms can be provided by excavating a basement, partitioning an existing room, or using adjoining homes or buildings, the opportunities for a graded program of worship and instruction will be increased.

2. *In Other Churches:* In our medium-sized and larger churches, where exclusive of the general church service of worship, all church school worship is usally on a divisional, departmental, or class basis, the superintendent does not customarily have direct responsibility for church school worship.

He should, however, be familiar with the practices within the school's graded worship program, and do everything possible to encourage the recognition of their value and importance. This will be true even in those larger churches that make use of a unified service of worship and study, and that emphasize the value of families attending the church worship service together as the foundation experience for the graded educational program of the church. Such a program does not require a general assembly of the school, as the church worship service is the school at worship, even as the class sessions are the church at study.

WORSHIP IN THE WORKERS' CONFERENCE

In Chapter 5 it was recommended that worship be included in every workers' conference program. The superintendent, as chairman of the workers' conference, is directly responsible for seeing that a worship service is planned and conducted as a regular part of the program. The superintendent can enhance the value of the worship in all of the church school departments through the emphasis he places on worship in the workers' conference. The worship service need not be long; usually ten to fifteen minutes is sufficient. It should, however, be prepared thoughtfully and with imaginative use of varied resources.

The workers' conference worship programs, therefore, become the superintendent's opportunity to provide not only a genuine worship experience, but also to demonstrate what worship is at its best. For these reasons, the worship services of the workers' conferences should be as carefully planned as the other parts of the program, and they should be in keeping with the theme. The superintendent should work closely with the program committee in preparation of the evening's program, including the worship.

The superintendent of the Sunday church school, whether the school be small or large, will find it wise to keep in mind that there are certain basic elements that contribute to effective worship. As he becomes increasingly familiar with these elements and discovers their unlimited possibilities for good, he will also realize how central worship is in the Christian education ministry of his school. He will be the better able also to counsel department superintendents and others respecting the improvement of worship.

WORSHIP ELEMENTS

include

ATTITUDES
SETTING
PROGRAM FACTORS
RESOURCE MATERIALS
CREATIVE IMAGINATION

THE ELEMENTS OF WORSHIP

1. *Attitudes:* Attitudes open the doors by which God enters our lives. Worship makes for better attitudes. The attitude of the worship leader will do much to determine the attitude of the other worshipers. We say, "We should be reverent," but what does true reverence involve?

Expectancy is a part of reverence. The conviction that the worship experience is real, that something significant is happening, and that we are privileged to share in it—all this is a part of true worship.

Receptiveness also is a part of true worship. The recognition that God is reaching out to us, even as we are reaching out to God, is basic. When this attitude is real, then worship is real.

Sincerity is fundamental to worship. There are few things, if any, that block so quickly the channel of fellowship with God as does insincerity. Sincerity of spirit makes it possible for worship to be genuine; and it must be genuine if it is to be helpful.

Commitment is implicit in worship. We worship God because basically we recognize as valid in all the other relationships of life the implications of our personal and group commitment. Worship is a constant renewal of that commitment to God.

Fulfillment is the outcome of worship. Whether we desire to share gratitude, to ask forgiveness, to gain strength, or to seek wisdom, worship finds its indication of effectiveness in fulfillment.

These, then, are the attitudes that create reverence, the mood for worship. If the worship leader exhibits them, he has a better opportunity of communicating them to others.

2. *Setting:* Because we are not disembodied spirits, we are influenced by the setting in which our experiences take place. This is true of worship; the setting is important.

The room, with its color, its lighting, its ventilation, its furniture, and its seating arrangement, is either depressing or conducive to worship. A room in order, neatly and attractively furnished, well-lighted but not glaring, well-ventilated but not drafty, is obviously an aid to those worshiping.

The worship center itself should be easily seen by all present. Whatever objects or symbols are used in it should be suitable to the worship theme and expressive of it. Religious pictures, the Bible, flowers, the cross, and candles are among the traditional symbols used.

The accessories, such as hymnals, musical instruments, reading stand or pulpit, and Bibles, should be kept in first-class condition. Hymnals with loose pages or broken covers, pianos with off-key notes, and littered tables obviously add in no way to the experience of worship, particularly for those new members or visitors not blinded or deafened by familiarity with them.

3. *Program Factors:* If worship is central to the spiritual vitality of the church's educational program, prayer is central to worship. Prayer may take many forms: silent prayer, brief prayers from several participants, spoken prayer by the leader or some designated person, and guided prayer. Prayer is evidence that we believe in the reality of our conscious relationship with God and are ready to share in it.

Hymns constitute another factor in programming for worship. With the large number of hymns available—hymns that cover a vast range of Christian experience—there is no reason to use any but the best. The hymnal, next to the Bible, will prove to be the superintendent's most versatile program resource. Hymns may be used in singing, in prayer, in commenting on Bible verses, and in the interpretation of Christian life and character. They may be sung, they may be read, they may be hummed, or they may be played instrumentally.

The Bible, of course, is the basic source book of our faith, and from its pages come passages of true inspiration and worship. Some passages are more suitable for worship than are others; some selections are more expressive of group aspirations than others; and obviously some sections relate to the worship theme more closely than do others. As the superintendent gains familiarity with his Bible, he will discover more sections that can be appropriately used in worship.

The interpretation of the worship theme may take any one of many forms. It may be a story, a poem, or a reading which is related to the Scripture passage; it may be a hymn, a solo, a duet, or an anthem; it may center in the worship symbol or picture; or it may be a brief message.

When an offering is included, it should definitely be considered an act of worship: an expression of dedication, commitment, and participation in some phase of God's purpose.

4. *Resource Materials:* In addition to the Bible and the hymnal, several other sources of worship materials are available. Some denominational magazines provide suggestions for workers' conference worship services, as well as for graded worship in the Sunday church school.

Devotional booklets, such as *The Secret Place, The Upper Room,* and *Today* frequently contain stories adaptable for worship services. The many devotional books which are constantly coming off the presses may be similarly used. In addition, there is a rapidly growing number of books specifically prepared as resource books for worship services.

Another growing field of worship resources is that of audio-visual aids. If these are used as aids to worship, they can be most helpful.

Even as the church library should include books and magazines to aid worship leaders in their planning, so the church school will find it helpful to build up a collection of mounted pictures, slides, records, tape-recorded aids, etc., that will be available when needed.

A different classification of resource materials lies within the Christian or church year itself. Christmas, Easter, Pentecost, Mother's Day, Children's Day, Father's Day, and our national holidays, all have a rich heritage of stories and customs that can contribute to the program of worship.

A final resource for effective worship lies within the various persons in your church who can share in the leadership of worship. When another person (child, youth, or adult) is asked to take part by reading the Scripture passage or by leading in prayer, the time taken to coach this participant to do his best will add much to the effectiveness of the service. Well-prepared persons are among the greatest worship resources a superintendent can use!

5. *Creative Imagination in Worship:* Almost every printed worship program will need adaptation, if it is to be of greatest value. Differences in physical equipment, setting, worship resources, individuals and groups, and the worship leaders themselves all condition what aids worship most in a specific situation. A recognition of this fundamental fact, together with a willingness to harness the imagination creatively can work wonders with even the most commonplace worship suggestions.

First, examine a suggested worship service and analyze it in the light of suggestions made earlier in this chapter. For a beginner in the art of worship program construction, this is usually, at first, a sounder approach than making a completely new program.

Second, in the light of the suggested worship theme, make the necessary changes in the program to fit your particular needs. You know your local situation and the group you are leading. Are there good hymns in your hymnal more apt than those suggested? As for the Scripture reading, do you know a more appropriate selection, or is there a more impressive way of including it in the service? Can it best be included as a solo reading, as a unison reading, or as a responsive reading? How helpful would it be to present it in the form of a litany or through a speech-choir rendering?

How can the prayer experience be made most vital to those participating in the service? Which will be the best procedure: a guided prayer, brief sentence prayers, silent prayer, prayer by the leader, or a combination of these?

Finally, how can the transition from the group experience to worship be made most effectively and smoothly? From worship to the next group experience? Does music help?

The search for answers to the above questions should stimulate the alert superintendent to use his creative imagination in improving the worship of the Sunday church school, thereby strengthening its spiritual life.

PERSONAL CONTACTS

Through his personal contacts, the superintendent can accomplish at least two things:

Through his contacts outside his own church, the superintendent can find out what other churches and church schools are doing. He can then adapt and make use of such discoveries as will improve the work of his own church school.

The superintendent also can encourage the members of his staff of workers to be on the alert for suggestions from others, and ask them to share these ideas in the workers' conference or staff meeting. From some of these suggestions may well come valuable additions to the church library for the use of all workers. Above all, however, there will come the realization that the spiritual vitality of the Sunday church school as communicated to its members must be the central concern of all the workers.

QUESTIONS AND PROJECTS

1. What is the responsibility of the superintendent in connection with the worship experience of a Sunday church school which is fully departmentalized? In a school with departments organized in the children's division only? In a one-room school?

2. Discuss worship as related to the Workers' Conference.

3. What elements are included in a good worship service?

4. Plan a service of worship for use with a group with which you are connected.

APPENDIX

A CURRICULUM PLAN FOR THE CHURCH SCHOOL[1]

God calls his church to mission, to share in reconciling to himself a separated world and people; to witness to the Good News of his redeeming love as revealed in the life, death, and resurrection of Jesus Christ.

The church ministers through functions of proclamation, teaching, worship, witness, fellowship, and service; and also in the administration of these functions. Each of the functions is related to the others and at the same time has a special ministry to fulfill in the total mission of the church.

The teaching ministry is designed to undergird all dimensions of the church's mission even as it in turn is undergirded by the other ministries. It is concerned with the process of teaching and learning, of disciplining the mind, of influencing the development of character through study and instruction, through action and reflection, and with equipping persons for informed participation in mission.

To avoid disorder and confusion in the teaching ministry it is necessary to design educational programs which give reasonable expectation that the church will be able to communicate its gospel and share its life. This provision for education is called a curriculum plan.

The curriculum plan described in this paper is for the "church school," one of several settings, all built upon the same foundation principles, interrelated and complementary, through which the church can attempt to fulfill its educational ministry. . . .

A BLUEPRINT FOR THE CHURCH SCHOOL

Ten elements describe the educational structure recommended for the church school:

1. a statement of the *purpose,* or a description of the *primary* contribution the church school makes to the church's overall mission,

[1] Approved by the Curriculum Committee of the American Baptist Churches January 10, 1968. This appendix contains only those parts of the document which would be of the broadest general interest.

89

2. the *constituency* of the church school, i.e., those persons for whose sake the church school is designed and administered,
3. the *grouping of persons* for teaching-learning in the church school,
4. the *frequency* with which groups meet for learning experiences,
5. the *time span for each meeting* or gathering of the teaching-learning groups,
6. the *location* of the group meetings,
7. the *leaders* required for operating the church school,
8. the *administration* of the church school,
9. the *duration* (or life-span) of a particular curriculum plan,
10. the *resources* for the church school as indicated by the curriculum plan.

Each of these elements influences the others and each is but one part of a total dynamic educational construct. The decisions made about each element serve as a guide to persons who want to provide Christian education opportunities by using the setting, the "church school." Below, each element is discussed in turn.

1. *The Primary Contribution of the Church School*

The primary contribution of the church school to the whole of the church's educational ministry is its focus upon and use of the disciplines and structures of a *school*. The church school offers persons, of whatever age, opportunities to engage in a regularly scheduled, year-round learning effort to understand and appropriate the meanings and experiences of the Christian faith and life. The church school program can help persons interrelate a wide range of issues, concerns, and responsibilities in light of:

1) an understanding of the Bible,
and
2) the insights of a Christian tradition that holds these concerns and responsibilities to be a primary means by which God reveals his truth to men.

Involvement in church school experiences is a systematic way by which persons can relate their persistent life concerns to the meaning and experiences of the gospel. It can also give them continuing guidance in living the Christian faith in the world as they grow in their awareness of God revealed in Jesus Christ, and as they respond to him in faith and love.

2. *Constituency of the Church School*

The church school is for persons of all ages. It includes both those who have responded to the call of Christ as his disciples, and those who are inquiring into the meaning of the Christian gospel but who have not yet committed themselves to it. Such an inclusive membership means that the church school will probably involve the largest number of learners of all settings in a church's educational ministry.

Under this curriculum plan, at the beginning of the church school year, persons will be asked to register for courses of study to be offered by the school that particular year. It should be made clear to the registrant (or his parents or guardian) that the school is designed for those who want to discover the meaning of the Christian gospel at the level of inquiry appropriate to their age. The act of registering will remind persons of the learning purpose of the school. After the beginning of the school year it will be necessary to provide for the enrollment and orientation of persons to the teaching-learning units already in process.

3. *Grouping in the Church School*

Grouping within the church school should be flexible and adaptable to:

   —the type of teaching facility available,
   —the ability, nature, and maturation of the students,
   —the commonalities of interests of persons who are potential members of learning groups
   —the training and experiences of the teachers or teaching teams.

Church school administrators should plan for each group to continue in existence only long enough to achieve its intended learnings; recognizing that too frequent regrouping can detract from the learning experience, while remaining over-long in one group can stultify it, particularly for youth and adults. Every group, regardless of its length of existence, should provide for maximum personal involvement.

In the graded series of the Christian Faith and Work Plan for the Church School the teaching-learning units from the kindergarten through the youth level are developed on a two-year grading plan and will most commonly be used with children and youth grouped by two school grades, and with younger children by groups organized on a two-year age span. Teaching-learning units in the uniform lesson series are more broadly graded.

It is recognized that in some congregations local factors may call for grouping by a single grade or age, or by as many as three grades or ages. Factors other than school grade, pre-elementary age, or post-school age may also be used as bases for grouping persons in the church school. These factors include: the learners' interests, concerns, talents, and abilities, growth, maturation, previous experiences, types of commitment, exceptional physical or mental capacities. Whatever the basis for grouping, the need for continuous teaching-learning of the Christian faith in groups goes on throughout life. The church school is designed to meet this need for all groups of all ages however related to the congregation.

The church school will use a variety of groupings: classes of learners, departments (groupings of classes), the total school, family or residential groups, teachers or leaders of classes, administrators and supervisors, and teachers and administrators. In the last three of these classifications, the ones dealing with church school leaders, the persons should sometimes be grouped as teachers or leaders of classes for the purpose of sharing common concerns and problems. Administrators and supervisors should come together at designated times to consider specific issues in their work. On occasion, church school teachers and administrators should form a single group to consider problems of concern to both.

4. *Frequency of Gatherings in the Church School*

While provision should be made for flexibility and adaptation, the curriculum plan proposes the following frequency of gatherings:

a. Classes for learners in the church school will meet at designated times once a week on a year-round basis, probably on Sunday morning. However, there is a growing trend for classes in the church school to meet at times other than Sunday morning.

b. Classes for persons who have had teaching experience and who wish to re-enter the church school faculty (and also for potential new leaders in the church school) should meet at designated times once a week on a year-round basis.

c. Groups of classes or the total school may meet for special purposes, though these meetings will probably be infrequent ones.

d. Leaders will have special meetings for training events supporting the church school.

Time Span of Gatherings in the Church School

It is essential that persons in any learning group have sufficient time for significant interchange, communication, and the development of relationships. The graded series in this curriculum plan has been designed to provide teaching-learning experiences based upon a time span of 60 to 120 minutes in recognition that longer sessions, under competent teachers, will contribute to more meaningful learning experiences. The uniform series in this curriculum plan has been designed for class session of from 45 to 60 minutes, recognizing that some churches must use the shorter period of time.

The length of time required for producing changes in understandings, attitudes, and action patterns will vary from church to church and from group to group. However, it is assumed that there are minimal time limits below which fruitful teaching-learning experiences are not likely to occur, just as there are terminal points beyond which teachers and pupils experience diminishing returns in learning for the time invested.

The longer periods for teaching-learning sessions using the Uniform Bible Series, the Faith and Work Graded Series, or the Bible and Life Graded Series for the Church School can provide the opportunity for quality education for pupils at every age level, and allow time for necessary maintenance tasks (such as taking attendance, making announcements, and creating a climate of friendliness and concern). The longer sessions also permit the entire school, or parts of it, to meet on special occasions to celebrate great events in the life of the church, or to share with one another some common themes and emphases within the teaching-learning units. In other situations the additional session time may be used for field trips and special study projects related to the congregations' educational ministry.

Children, perhaps more than youth and adults, are affected negatively by pressure, which often results when insufficient time is allowed for learning experiences in their church school groups. For this reason an increasing number of churches have moved the church school sessions for children to a weekday or Saturday, where they may have an uninterrupted period of two or two-and-one-half hours. Most churches, however, continue to feel that Sunday morning provides their best opportunity to reach the greatest number of children, and many have established an "Expanded Session" time for their learning. Usually, this "expanded" period is two hours or more long, and covers both the time set for the adult classes and for the

93

morning worship services of the church. The expanded session is single, unified session, with a *single* purpose and all activities, in cluding worship, are planned to contribute to that purpose.

6. *Location, or Places of Gathering for the Church School*

Groups of the church school will usually meet in the chur building, but may meet in other locations such as homes or retre centers. The congregation should provide facilities that imply mee ings for a school, for study; and which foster an atmosphere of e pectancy that "important learning happens here."

7. *Leadership in the Church School*

Designated leaders in the church school include those who teac those who supervise and administer (such as superintendents an other officers), and those who are called on for special resourc (music, art, drama, etc.). The minister(s) of the congregatio (pastor, minister of Christian education, and other associate mi isters) is/are seen as the ones carrying primary responsibility f leading and teaching the other designated leaders of the chur school. The minister(s) is the congregation's chief theologic resource person and is the teacher of church school leaders.

Leaders or teachers with special skills and abilities should be co missioned to help other teachers improve the quality and effectiv ness of their teaching, and should assist the pastor in giving leade ship to events and meetings related to these concerns. In additio resource persons from the community or beyond may from time time lead in the various training events for leaders.

The congregation has a responsibility to minister to the perso selected for designated leadership in its church school. This minist should touch their personal faith as well as their assigned teachi tasks. Most often this ministry to church school leaders will ta place within the local congregation; sometimes there will be lead development events sponsored by two or more churches within a association. All designated leaders in the church school should r ceive training before their appointment and during their time service.

8. *The Administration of the Church School*

The administration of the church school is the responsibility persons commissioned for this task by the congregation. General church school administration will be a part of the work directed l a congregation's board or committee of Christian education. A

94

arning groups within the church will operate within the policies
t by this administrative committee or board.

It is important to note that the educational efficiency of any
urch school is dependent upon the wise administrative policy of
board of Christian education. Effective curriculum throughout a
urch school grows from administrative policies on leadership de-
lopment, curriculum plans, curriculum materials, in this order.
fective curriculum occurs when administrative policies for Chris-
an education permit teachers to respond to the interests and needs
their pupils, joining the teachers' concerns with those of the
arners in the search for meanings in God's revelation.

Duration of the Church School Curriculum

While the church school will exist as long as congregations orga-
ze themselves to provide persons with systematic nurture in the
hristian faith, any one particular curriculum plan for the church
hool will be used for a definite, limited period of time. The cur-
culum plan now being developed as "The Christian Faith and
ork Plan for the Church School" will be in existence for nine
ars, beginning in September 1969. . . .

(For information concerning all ABC curriculum including the new Bible
d Life Graded Series, write to the Curriculum Services Department, American
ptist Churches, Valley Forge, Pa. 19481.)

Philip A. Anderson, *Church Meetings that Matter* (Philadelph: United Church Press, 1965).

Kenneth D. Blazier, *Building an Effective Church School* (Valle Forge: Judson Press, 1976).

Kenneth D. Blazier and Joseph John Hanson, *Launching the Chur School Year* (Valley Forge: Judson Press, 1972).

Kenneth D. Blazier and Evelyn M. Huber, *Planning Christi Education in Your Church* (Valley Forge: Judson Press, 1974).

Kenneth L. Cober, *Shaping the Church's Educational Ministry* (Val Forge: Judson Press, 1971).

Kenneth L. Cober, *The Church's Teaching Ministry* (Valley For Judson Press, 1964).

E. Weldon Keckley, *The Church School Superintendent: the Pers and the Job* (St. Louis: The Bethany Press, 1963).

Martha M. Leypoldt, *Forty Ways to Teach in Groups* (Valley For Judson Press, 1967).

George E. Riday, *Understanding the Learner* (Valley Forge: Juds Press, 1964).

Paul H. Vieth, *The Church School* (Philadelphia: United Chur Press, 1957).